Constructual Marital Therapy

DEAR LINDA,
 MANY COUPLES WILL COME TO YOU WITH THEIR
HOPES AND JOY. I HOPE THIS BOOK WILL ASSIST
YOU IN YOUR WORK WITH THEM.

With Love
Manbl

Constructual Marital Therapy

*Theory
and
Practice*

MARSHALL JUNG, D.S.W.

GARDNER PRESS, INC.
New York   London   Toronto   Sydney

The case material presented in this book consists of examples;
they do not reflect specific couples or individuals.

Library of Congress Cataloging in Publication Data
Jung, Marshall.
   Constructual marital therapy : theory and practice / Marshall
Jung.
        p.   cm.
   Includes bibliographical references and index.
   ISBN (invalid) 08987601913 : $29.95
   1. Marital psychotherapy.   I. Title.
RC488.5.J85   1993
619.89'156—dc20   92-34219
                                                   CIP

9 8 7 6 5 4 3 2

DEDICATION

This book is dedicated to my late father and mother,

Mr. and Mrs. How Jung, who shared a covenant marriage,

to my wife's parents, Mr. and Mrs. Jock Nay Wong,

who have loved me as their own son, and to Rosie,

who has been my loving devoted spouse

for twenty-seven years.

獻辭

謹將此書獻與先父省財及先母朱夫人，聊報養育之恩；其次獻與岳父黃惠世伉儷，以感戴其愛護之情，猶如己出；最後獻與共同生活廿七載之愛妻美比。

CONTENTS

Part IV: Case Presentations

LIST OF
DIAGRAMS
AND TABLES

PREFACE

THE IDEAS AND BELIEFS PRESENTED in this book are derived from my eighteen years of experience in practicing, teaching, supervising, and training in marital therapy. I have integrated into my practice those lessons I have learned from sociology, psychology, philosophy, anthropology and religion, and those lessons I learned from my clients. I am inviting you to examine my model, Constructual Marital Therapy, to take from it what you find useful in your practice, and to develop further concepts you find helpful.

Constructual Marital Therapy provides a structure, an orderly plan designed to rebuild a marriage to its greatest potential. Rebuilding includes reinforcing the foundation, refurbishing and restoring the worn and fragile places that occur in the absence of nurturing maintenance. But it is not enough for a structure to be restored to beauty. It must have occupants who will treasure and maintain the establishment.

The structure is the body of the relationship. Constructual Marital Therapy addresses the body of the marriage. The occupants are the heart of the marriage. The "covenant relationship" addresses the heart of the marriage. The "covenant relationship" is my description of the kind of marriage I believe all loving couples hope to achieve.

Mature marriage is the uniting of two human beings who wish to fulfill their love by developing and maintaining a mutually enhancing relationship. The marriage will be greatly influenced by what each partner brings to it. Therefore, I found it necessary to address the issue of individual psychological development. I have built my analysis of personal growth and development out of what I believe to be of primary importance to the individual—the presence of an intrinsic human dignity. This quality of human dignity is God's gift to us and is what allows us to establish and maintain autonomy and loving relationships.

The concept of a "covenant relationship" and the importance of human dignity form the foundation of this book. These two factors are behind my ideas regarding individual and marital growth and development, the reasons couples have difficulty in establishing and maintaining happy marriages, my treatment goals, and therapeutic techniques and principles of practice.

Constructual marital therapists must have solid training and carefully developed technical skills. The practitioner must never lose sight that marital therapy is an interactional process and that we are being allowed a privileged place in people's lives. Our clients, at the most vulnerable times in their lives, trust us with their deepest feelings, their hope and their pain in the belief that we will be able to help them make major life decisions. The feelings that are offered must be handled with the greatest gentleness and dignity. We must respect our clients, be sensitive to their pain, and recognize that we are there to help, not to judge. A therapist must possess more than technical skill. There must be a recognition of the inherent strength and goodness in every human beings.

My daughter, Eileen, recently asked me, "Don't you get depressed, hearing people's problems all day? How do you manage not to feel overwhelmed after a day's work?" I answered that when I feel overwhelmed, it is not usually by the problems people present to me. I am constantly overwhelmed by seeing the courage that people possess, their inner strength, and their compassion and dignity in times of excruciating personal pain and life–threatening problems.

It is seeing the spark of human dignity illuminating terrible darknesses which has motivated me to write this book.

ACKNOWLEDGMENTS

THERE WERE MANY PEOPLE who contributed to supporting me in the writing of this book. I am especially indebted to my dear friend and editor Ms. Rowena Silver. We spent untold hours working together on the manuscript. I am also indebted to my spiritual director, Father Michael Sweeney, O.P., who unselfishly allowed me to use his concepts of a covenant marriage. I owe a special thanks to my friends and colleagues, Dr. John and Mrs. Mary Daley, who supported me both personally and professionally in so many ways. Among other things, they read my manuscript and offered many helpful editorial comments. Three other colleagues who read my manuscript and gave me helpful ideas were Dr. Frances Caple, Dr. Helen Land, and Mrs. Nancy Steiny. Finally, I am grateful to the many colleagues and students who allowed me to influence their professional development. Special among them are Ms. Sue Bloomfield, Ms. Elizabeth Garigan, Dr. William W. Hillman, Ms. Carol J. Hollander, and Ms. Lee Keaton.

I

Introduction

1
FOUNDATION FOR MARRIAGE

CONSTRUCTUAL MARITAL THERAPY (CMT) is a complex, comprehensive and pragmatic model of therapy designed to help couples in conflict. Constructual is derived from the Latin word, construct, meaning—"to build up" and this is exactly what the model does; in a systematic manner it builds upon and integrates various theoretical concepts and models of practice. The model describes steps toward a happy and successful modern relationship. It is defined here as "the covenant marriage." We show what is required in the stages of marital development through which couples must pass in order to achieve such a relationship. We classify the problems encountered by couples on their journey toward fulfillment into five broad categories for examination and treatment.

Principles of practice and the rationale from which they were derived are presented for use in clinical interventions. Clear guidelines are developed for working with couples to determine whether it is appropriate to use conjoint, concurrent, collaborative or combined therapy. Five interconnecting paradigms within which marital therapy can be conducted are offered. Within each feature of the CMT framework we draw from those models of practice and theory which we deem appropriate for conceptualizing, diagnosing, planning or intervening. The model allows freedom for therapists to select from their own body of knowledge and experience in theoretical concepts and principles of practice which leads couples to travel together on a clear and harmonious path.

FOUNDATION FOR MARRIAGE

Most marital therapists agree that one requirement of a mutually enhancing relationship is that each partner has achieved a state of psychological maturity. Therapeutic interventions are directed at fundamental issues critical to establishing and enhancing a relationship. These interventions include: helping couples better understand one another, improving communication and problem solving skills, learning to accept and integrate differences, and resolving family of origin issues. The interventions made and the issues addressed are dependent upon the theoretical orientation of the therapist.

Three major approaches to marital therapy are: psychodynamic, behavioral, and systems. The theoretical formulations and underpinnings of each of these approaches are highly valuable and contribute a great deal to the understanding of marital dynamics. However, each approach has its limitations. Some of the methods focus too narrowly upon either the intrapsychic process of each spouse, the behaviors they exhibit, or their interpersonal dynamics. There is often a lack of recognition that there are normally multiple causal factors contributing to the development of marital relationships. More important, it is often the case that the literature of marital therapy does not address societal and cultural influences on marriage, the question of what marriage is, the role of love in marital development and what couples expect marriage to be. I have attended several workshops on marital therapy where the presenters never discussed their ideas about what marriage is, what love is, and what couples honestly want in a marital relationship.

The statistic that ninety percent of Americans will marry[1] indicates that a large majority of people still believe that marital happiness is possible. Everyone who gets married willingly does so in the expectation that this is where happiness and fulfillment will be achieved. Most learn that their expectations of what a marriage should be are never realized. This is evidenced by the divorce rate of modern marriages of forty-five percent and of those couples who remain together, a large percentage are unhappy in the relationship. Given that millions of Americans will not achieve a successful marriage, we must view these statistics as a social problem and examine those factors in society which influence the expectations and development of marriage.

A section of this book will address these factors. However, I believe that the most significant one is that although most couples desire a mutually nurturing relationship they do not understand the complexities involved in establishing and maintaining a happy marriage. Until the recent past, marriage was based upon traditional values. Roles were clearly defined and therefore couples knew how to build a relationship. Today, marriage is based on "love" and the democratic principle of equal rights. As a result, relationships are often based on a vague concept of what "love" is and a resultant lack of clarity as to what should and can be enhancing to a marriage.

Given the above, I wish to begin by presenting a working definition of what I believe to be the elements of a happy marriage: Marriage is the institution that is established when two individuals, whose names are at stake, come together freely, out of love, seeking union for its own sake. By defining the concepts in this definition I hope to clarify some of the confusion couples experience in regard to marital expectation and to provide the theoretical formulations upon which CMT is based.

I have arrived at this definition of a good marriage through years of work with couples in therapy, the theoretical formulations of others, my experiences as a spouse, and my value system.

2

MARRIAGE AS
AN INSTITUTION

WHEN MARRYING, couples often fail to recognize that they are establishing an institution—an organization having social, education and/or religious purpose. As an institution, marriage is one of the building blocks upon which a society is established and maintained.

> A society exists to provide collectively for the fundamental needs of its members. A society would be unable to continue its existence if it did not provide for the production and distribution of goods, protect itself from its enemies, and regulate the differences and quarrels of its neighbors. In addition, a society must provide for orderly methods of reproduction, nurturing, and socializing children if it is to persist beyond the first generation.[2]

The institution of marriage begins with a legal contract which legitimatizes the expected permanence of a relationship between two people. With the contract comes legal obligations which are not generally addressed or even recognized unless there is a pending divorce. The marriage and contract are usually recorded in a formal religious or civil ceremony.

Each spouse must share responsibility in the marriage. In the past, these responsibilities were dictated by traditional norms and values. Traditional marriages were based upon functions, and roles were clearly defined and prescribed. The roles reflected the social values and customs of the community. Often, marriages were arranged for the mutual benefit of the extended families. The marital dyad itself was an extension of the family. One did not marry an individual person, but rather "married into" a family. The family was seen as in integral part of the community. As a result, the marriage ceremony has historically been a family and community event.

At a recent Chinese marriage I attended, there were about four hundred guests present. These guests were family and friends of the bride and groom, and delegated representatives from the community. Couples lived with or maintained close ties with their families of origin, from which they received support, guidance and social intercourse. Spouses in such traditional marriages did not have difficulty negotiating differences, as they came from the same background and had similar social values, economic goals, ethnic heritage, and expectations from marriage. Finally, the traditional marriage was highly structured and satisfied the needs of the extended family. Emphasis was on the "we" and not on the "I." Satisfaction from such relationships was achieved when the programmed expectations of marriage were fulfilled.

The institution of marriage has changed dramatically in recent years. In the modern marriage, responsibility is negotiable and not dictated by tradition. In fact, each couple decides the kind of relationship they want, the goals they would like to achieve, and the means by which they will reach these goals.

Modern marriage is based on love and the roles are not clearly defined. The marital dyad is seen as an entity in itself and couples often find themselves distanced from family of origin. Couples move into a community, but most of their social, psychological and recreational needs are met elsewhere. The marriage ceremony itself might even be private—a quick trip to Las Vegas or to a Justice of the Peace. Modern couples are often self-reliant and take the initiative to establish their own support systems. In modern marriage, it is common for the couple to have major differences in philosophy, culture, religion, values and attitudes toward parenting. Emphasis is not on the extended "we" but rather on the narrow nuclear "we" and on the "I." Marriage has become, in part, a process of negotiating differences. Finally, modern marriages have expectations of equality and thus require enormous flexibility. Satisfaction from such a relationship is achieved when both partners believe that their individual needs are being met.

TWO INDIVIDUALS

A marital relationship begins when two individuals decide to become an integral part of each others' lives. I agree with those theoreticians who believe that individuals tend to match at about the same psychological maturity level. I also believe that, given a reasonable level of attained maturity on the part of both spouses, each can help the other to better understand themselves and their psychological insecurities. This helps both mature more fully, while at the same time builds trust and makes the relationship more enriching. However, if the partners are immature, they will have great difficulty being supportive and attentive to one another's needs. If, for example, we measure maturity on a scale of one to ten, ten being most mature, those with a maturity level of seven or eight will have a much easier job helping their partner to grow emotionally than those beginning at a maturity scale of two or three. The more immature an individual is, the more selfish they will be and the more they will try to meet their own needs before addressing the needs of their partner. Maturity and autonomy are necessary elements of an enhancing marriage.

WHOSE NAMES ARE AT STAKE

In this book, name means more than the proper noun assigned to a person at birth. It refers to the essence of "who I am." That essence is more than what I can adequately describe about myself. I can, for example, describe myself in terms of my personality characteristics, beliefs, values, areas of interest, and many other things. The essence of who I am, however, is the gestalt of all of these factors. Like love, the concept of who I am is absolutely clear to me, but never fully describable. Furthermore, who I am is in a constant state of evolution. This is one of the reasons that marriage is the most profound relationship that I can enter. It, as much as I will let it, will influence not only the direction my life will take, but the person that I will ultimately become.

The following case example illustrates how dramatically one spouse can influence the other.

Janet, a 35-year-old physician, was seen by me due to severe marital difficulties. Her marriage began with love and her expectation that she and her husband would develop a mutually enhancing relationship. In the early years of the marriage she had had a positive self-concept and she believed that she had good self-knowledge. At the time of therapy, Janet's friends, colleagues, family and this therapist saw her as a giving, respectful, sensitive, responsible and reasonable individual. Her husband, however, was extremely critical of her. He accused her of being insensitive, selfish, unreasonable and incompetent. She realized that she could exhibit such characteristics, but at a deeper level she did not accept her husband's description. On one level of awareness, she believed him, but on another she did not. She had difficulty discerning herself because of the continual negative messages she received from him.

COME TOGETHER FREELY

Freedom illuminates dignity because it allows for the freedom to express and the freedom to be. In marriage, when we choose freely to seek union, the union begins with dignity as well as love. I come to the relationship freely wishing to share with you the essence of myself, and hoping that you will share the essence of yourself with me. This wish is generally unconscious, but at some level I am willing to give up some liberties so that a mutually enhancing relationship can develop.

By allowing ourselves to share with one another we can perpetuate the concept of freedom. In sharing, we invite, we do not demand, that our partner attend to whom we are. We encourage our partner to exercise freedom of choice.

With marriage comes the implicit understanding that the relationship will be exclusive and that the partners will be faithful to each other. Partners give up the right to act independently and defer to joint decision making. This allows each spouse to participate in the relationship equally and with the freedom to express thoughts and beliefs.

Unfortunately, some individuals believe that marriage is a contract which sets limits on the freedom of their partner and on themselves. As a result, couples will develop a pattern of interaction whereby they knowingly or unknowingly attempt to change the other's behaviors, beliefs, or values. Thus, controlling behavior and dependency is what is fostered, rather than freedom and autonomy.

The desire to control a partner's behavior is often initiated with good intentions. In a recent interview, for example, John expressed to his wife, Susan, his tremendous unhappiness and frustration over the fact that he felt smothered by her attempts to control his behavior. She ignored his statement of feeling, and minimized his concerns by telling him how much he had grown and how his interests in life had broadened. She concluded by announcing that she was going to make him the best person he could be. She did not recognize her controlling behavior and believed that she was acting in his best interests. But what she was doing was depriving him of the right to be himself. The relationship was based on a concept that she was the benevolent parent and he the needy child. Freedom was lost in the relationship.

I believe freedom must be allowed throughout a marriage, one aspect of which is the freedom to choose to stay or leave the marriage. Accompanying this belief is the concept that part of the marital process is a continuous recommitment to the relationship. Unfortunately, the notion of recommitment is normally only recognized when couples seek therapy, or when they renew their vows after twenty–five or fifty years of marriage. I suggest to couples I see that they recommit to each other at every wedding anniversary.

I recognize that there are couples who enter therapy knowing their marriage will never be happy but believe they have no choice but to remain no matter how dysfunctional or destructive the relationship. This belief might be based on religious, cultural and/or family values. In such cases, I assist the partners in examining their values. If they still conclude they must stay in the relationship, I assist them in making the best out of a difficult and unhappy situation. In so doing, I help them to realize that they remain in the marriage out of obligation and not freedom and that they must accept this if they are to find peace and resolution. How this is accomplished, and the usual outcome of such relationships is discussed in the section "Constructual Marital Therapy Paradigms."

The loss of freedom in a marriage is due, in part, to couples confusing the concepts of "hope" and "expectation." Partners stop "hoping" but rather "expect" that their needs will be met. But it is hope, not expectation, which facilitates an interactional pattern based on warmth and understanding. Expectation implies a duty to act, invites feelings of indebtedness, and ends in a stagnant relationship which is based on bargaining. Hope, on the other hand, invites loving gestures, encourages partners to give freely, and moves toward a relationship of mutual enhancement.

It is instinctive to want to take control in a relationship because we are not taught to be comfortable in helplessness. There are many reasons why one person will want to control another but the attempt to do so will always prevent or stagnate freedom. It is helpful for partners to learn to influence rather than to attempt to control. Influence is best accomplished by example, and by having real knowledge of the partner's strengths and needs. In influencing, partners allow each other the freedom to share beliefs, make decisions, and manifest who they are.

OUT OF LOVE

Most modern couples marry out of feelings of love. When we ask spouses what the word "love" means, most have difficulty defining this concept, upon which they have made their most important life decision. Most will describe a special feeling or confuse it with concepts of trust, respect or friendship. I tell these couples that one is able to trust, respect and be friends with a variety of people, and yet not love them. I believe that it is vital for couples to have a clearly defined idea of what love is, so that they will be able to use this concept to facilitate a process where their love can have a deeper meaning and upon which their marriage can grow in a mutually enhancing way.

Love occurs naturally. It cannot be made to happen. Love must be given and received freely; it is something that cannot be purchased. Partners come together freely, seeking to learn more about one another and to enjoy the unique experiences that are part of the relationship.

I believe that love is experienced in the same way that we experience the world—cognitively, affectively, behaviorally, and, for some, spiritually. First, I experience the world cognitively, therefore love is a belief. People who are in love usually know that they are in love even if there are times when they are not in touch with loving feelings. Love is concrete, but never fully describable. When two people experience love, there is a sudden cognitive awareness of that fact which cannot always be articulated. I know I am in love, and can describe many thoughts and feelings about my belief. I can say, for example, that I love her because she is intelligent, kind and assertive. But I can describe those characteristics in others whom I do not love. The awareness of my love can only be known to me as I take into consideration the totalness of my partner. There is the absolute knowledge that "This is the person for whom I have been waiting all my life."

Second, I experience the world affectively, therefore love is a special feeling that I experience, but cannot fully describe. For most people, love is experienced as an overpowering and burning feeling. It is also experienced as a unique feeling which I have for my "other." This is not to say I cannot have loving feelings for others, but it is not the same. The full experience of love is never felt continuously. We have to go to work, take out the garbage, argue with relatives and pay the bills. At times I might even feel angry, resentful, or even hateful toward my loved one. That is why it is important that I know that I love my partner. If love were to be defined only in terms of feeling, there would be no continuity and we would be able to turn love on and off like a kitchen faucet. Although we cannot experience the feeling of love continuously, these feelings are filed away at a preconscious or subconscious level where we are able to access them and act on them when it is situationally appropriate.

Third, because we experience the world behaviorally, love must be manifested in behavior. Most couples recognize that love cannot be proven, but must be demonstrated through loving gestures such as words, actions and gifts. Lovers have the need to be attentive to the needs and wishes of their partners. For most couples, the greatest gesture of love is the making of sacrifices—one to the other—and only for the sake of the other. Such gestures send a profound and clear message to the receiver that they are truly loved. Thus, loving gestures reinforce the belief that I love and am loved, which amplifies the special feelings associated with being in love, which reinforces my desire to make loving gestures. In later examples, we will demonstrate how such gestures are required in the establishment of a covenant relationship.

Finally, some people experience the world spiritually and therefore express their love through their religious experiences. Their beliefs transcend the couple and connect them to the wonders of life and is felt as a gift of God.

SEEKING

When couples commit to a marriage they seek to fulfill their love by building an enhancing relationship. They hope that their love will continue to grow and that they will always be nurtured and supported in the marriage. Being together is paramount and they hope to stay together all their lives. In being together, they wish to share new adventures, and they usually hope to raise a family. Spouses want to know each other in greater depth and to share their inner selves. In so doing, trust and intimacy are experienced.

There are times when partners stop seeking union. An important reason this happens is that often there is a failure of the couple to realize there are no limits to the degree to which a loving relationship can grow. Some couples are limited when they develop a dependent relationship, when they become complacent and stop working toward enhancement. In any case, the relationship becomes dull, stagnant and perhaps even empty. Rather than being part of an energizing force, partners settle into a life of boring routine. If this occurs, loving gestures are not made and if they are, they are taken for granted. Partners turn to others for entertainment and enhancement, or they begin to expect their partner to "make them happy."

To seek means to try to find, or to search for. Seeking implies forward movement, newness, excitement, exploration, challenge, vitality —in short, positive and creative energy. If we continue to seek union the relationship does not stagnate, but rather new avenues for expression, enjoyment and mutual growth can be achieved on a continuous basis. Seeking provides a perpetual hope for an ever enhancing marriage.

I encourage couples to continue to seek union with one another. I often recommend marital enrichment workshops or programs such as marriage encounters to assist them in obtaining the knowledge and skills to continue to build a loving relationship. I also suggest several things that they can do to attend to their marriage, such as taking vacations alone, spending time together daily, and continuing to make enhancing gestures to one another.

UNION

In modern marriages, individuals bond together to develop a relationship in which they form a union, becoming part of one another and at the same time maintaining autonomy. Many theoreticians characterize this relationship as having three components, the husband, wife and the "we." Eric Fromm describes this process:

> ". . . mature love is union under the condition of preserving one's integrity, one's individuality. Love is an active power in man; a power which breaks through the walls which separate man from his fellow men, which unites him with others; love makes him overcome the sense of isolation and separateness, yet it permits him to be himself, to retain his integrity. In love the paradox occurs that two beings become one yet remain two."[3]

In this work we will define this bonding as the "we psyche."

The "we psyche" is the emotional state of inter–connectedness experienced by spouses which, under usual conditions, begins when they "fall in love" and becomes progressively stronger as the relationship develops and becomes more exclusive. The bond of interconnectedness is intensified when the couples marry or move in together, as they then begin to eat, sleep and think "we." Everything that they will do, where they will go, immediate and long range plans, expenditure of monies, etc. will be negotiated within and will be based upon the new relationship. The longer the couple stays together, the stronger the "we psyche" will become.

In addition to the length of time the couple is together, the development of the "we psyche" is influenced by the conditions of the

Diagram I
Types of Marriage

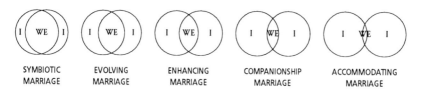

marriage and the degree of autonomy each spouse displays. Diagram 1 illustrates the "we psyche" continuum.

At one end of the continuum there is the accommodation marriage in which there is little sense of "we" bondedness, but a strong sense of self. In such relationships, spouses do not marry or stay married for love, but rather for practical purposes such as saving money, religious belief, or to protect children from the pain of divorce. Spouses are autonomous and adhere to the reasons why they remain married. Neither expects or wishes any nurturance, emotional support or care from the other. Such needs are met outside the marriage. In effect, the spouses live separate lives and only come together to satisfy practical needs.

Further along the continuum, there is the companionship marriage which is based on mutual friendship rather than love. There is a moderate amount of "we" bondedness. Like accommodating marriages, spouses remain together for practical reasons. The marriage might have begun under these conditions, or it might have evolved into them. For example, I worked with a couple who initially married twenty-five years ago for love. Both were mature people, but each was dissatisfied with the marriage at the time of treatment. Upon examination of the relationship, the husband recognized that during the integration stage of marital development, he had drifted emotionally away from his wife and he no longer loved her. She, however, remained in love with him. They had raised three children and the youngest was now preparing to move out to attend college. The couple agreed that they had remained good friends, enjoyed mutual interests, and had a common network of friends. They respected and trusted one another. They also agreed that although the relationship was not completely fulfilling there were enough positive attributes to the marriage that they could receive satisfaction, even happiness from it. They decided to remain together.

At the center of the continuum there is the enhancing marriage which is a balance of sense of self and we bondedness. The enhancing marriage is founded on freedom and mutual love. Spouses enter the marriage with autonomy or it develops as the marriage matures. As a result, they are able to create a happy relationship by sharing intimacy and being mutually supportive and loving.

Further along the continuum is the evolving marriage. This relationship is based on mutual love, however the couple has unresolved insecurities in one or both partners or in the relationship. There is a strong sense of "we" bondedness at the expense of the partners' autonomy. As a result, the couple remains primarily in the bargaining stage of marital development. Spouses find it difficult to give freely and they want their partner to change for them. They have difficulty accepting differences, continue to disagree about who is in control of the relationship and frequently complain about not being understood, validated or nurtured. Profound trust and friendship are not developed. However, when there is a lack of conflict, the couple recognize and experience the love they have for one another. They enjoy each others' company and are enriched by plans of building a future together. As the spouses mature they move further toward an enhancing relationship.

At the other end of the continuum there is the symbiotic marriage. Here there is great "we" bondedness but little sense of self. In such marriages, couples have often married for practical reasons. However, unlike those couples in an accommodating marriage, these spouses lack autonomy and have often married to meet psychological dependency needs. Such partners might have married to get away from the parental home, for financial security, or because they believe that they will have little choice in mate selection. Although they initially married to meet dependency needs, they recognize and desire what is normally hoped for in a marriage; mutual support, validation and nurturance. As a result of their immaturity and lack of love, such couples will establish a conflictual marriage leading to a further loss of dignity and self in the relationship.

Many couples establish symbiotic marriages even though they married for love and hope for a mutually enhancing relationship. However, due to a lack of autonomy, they are not able to give of themselves, which leads to a relationship based upon little acceptance of the other and attempts at controlling. The attempts to control the relationship facilitates an interactional process in which the spouses inevitably lose dignity, and finally lose themselves in the relationship.

Often, spouses who are unhappy will make statements suggesting that there is no inter-connectedness in the relationship. This is reflected in such statements as "I feel nothing toward him." But the sense of lack of inter-connectedness is rarely true. What they usually mean is that there is no love or there are no shared positive feelings. They have no awareness of the power of the we aspect of the relationship or understanding how it can be manifested, positively or negatively. When the we psyche is experienced negatively, partners will feel misunderstood, rejected, discounted or unloved. This will often lead to arguments, rigid behavior, lack of freedom and attempts to control the relationship. In extremely dysfunctional, symbiotic relationships there will be verbal and/or physical abuse which can be so destructive as to lead to one partner killing the other. But when the we psyche is experienced positively, partners will feel support, concern for one another and profound intimacy. Such couples show each other respect, demonstrate kindness, consideration and independence. In exceptionally enhancing relationships, the partners would give up their lives for the other.

In enhancing relationships, the we psyche is the state of togetherness in which each spouse believes him/herself to be complete. On the surface it would appear that the two concepts—autonomy and unity—are paradoxical. How can the couple develop a we psyche and at the same time develop autonomy? This state of completeness is manifested, for example, when a partner makes a statement such as, "I feel amplified, as if I were more than I was—more powerful than when I was alone."

The paradox of the we psyche is reflected by questions such as "How much am I willing to give of myself to meet the needs of the relationship? How responsible am I for the needs of my spouse? How much of my own identity am I willing to give up?" The apparent paradox is resolved if couples are able to establish a mutually enhancing relationship.

FOR ITS OWN SAKE

For its own sake means that each partner comes or remains in the marriage for no other reason but as a gift to the partner and to work toward an enhancing relationship. There are no hidden agendas. If this is true, the marriage will be based primarily on love, freedom, respect and friendship. This does not negate the need for financial security, stability, companionship and the need to be cared for. These needs are part of what a marriage requires and they ought to be met. However these needs are window–dressing, not the foundation upon which a marriage should be built. The concept of marriage out of pure love seems idealistic to some, but it is not—it is concrete. Couples are capable of having such relationships, and I have never known a couple who did not want this kind of marriage.

3

THE COVENANT RELATIONSHIP

A COVENANT RELATIONSHIP is established when the criteria in the working definition of a happy marriage are met, that is, when two individuals, whose names are at stake, come together freely, to seek union for it own sake. These criteria are not always in place when partners exchange marriage vows. More often than not the marital relationship evolves into a covenant one rather than beginning as one. Two individuals might, for example, come together initially to meet dependency needs, but later discover the deep love they have for one another. At this time the foundation upon which the marriage was built is changed. The marriage might change due to psychological insecurities and become a symbiotic relationship when little freedom, autonomy or dignity is manifested. Later, with maturity, or with the assistance of therapy, the partners are able to develop their autonomy, reclaim their dignity and allow freedom to be manifested in the relationship.

In a covenant relationship the partners develop an interactional pattern in which, on a conscious or unconscious level, they allow the other to influence their emotional growth and development by becoming "loving witnesses" to one another. By their ability to share their thoughts and feelings about one another the spouses can acquire greater understanding about themselves, their partners and their relationship. This in turn allows couples to achieve a greater depth of nurturance, intimacy and support.

A covenant relationship begins with two autonomous people

coming together freely, with their dignity intact, and seeking union for its own sake. In so doing, each asks the other, "Will you share a life of love and happiness with me?" In giving to one another freely, the marital event is dignified and so provides a strong structural basis on which the marriage can build. Giving oneself freely also implicitly states that each partner is relinquishing freedom to some degree and wishes to be responsible for the well–being of the other.

Couples in a covenant relationship feel and express to each other, "I have called you into my life—I am placing my destiny at stake and allowing you to influence the essence of my being. Not only is the future of our relationship to be determined by this union but also the person I am to become." Profound trust is thus required of the partners.

The covenant is achieved in marriages where partners are at some level of awareness, willing to place their future identity at risk in the relationship. This is often not the case when couples marry for reasons such as wanting to leave the parental home or feelings of obligation due to pregnancy. In such cases, the future of the partners is not addressed. Instead, what is of primary importance is, in the first case, escape from a negative home environment and in the second, the need to fulfill a responsibility. The fact that the very destiny of two separate people will become interconnected is rarely considered.

By allowing my partner to influence the essence of my being, I hope that he/she will understand, validate, accept and delight in knowing and being with me. More importantly, I wish to understand, validate, accept and be delighted in knowing him/her. It is for this reason that it is in marriage, more than any other relationship, that the individual will feel most hurt by feelings of being misunderstood and invalidated. When one partner says to the other, "I don't know why you cry all the time," there is an expressed lack of understanding. If the partner says instead, "I wish you would stop being so sensitive and stop crying," there is some understanding, but no validation. When the observation is, "You're so damned sensitive, but if I'm going to continue in the marriage, I guess I'll have to put up with it," there is understanding and acceptance (actually accommodation, which is a form of acceptance), but no enhancement. If however, the partner says, "I love your sensitivity, especially when I see it shown in your empathy"—implied is, "I know, validate and accept you."

In a covenant relationship spouses hope that their partners will be attentive to their well being because the foundation of the marriage is love. Unfortunate couples confuse the concept of hope with the concept of expectation. As a result, hopefulness is lost and marriages are then based primarily upon meeting mutual expectations. However it is hope, rather than expectation, which facilitates an interactional pattern based on mutual warmth and enrichment. Expectation implies duty, encourages feelings of indebtedness and begets a stagnant relationship which is based on bargaining. Hope, on the other hand, invites loving gestures, encourages partners to freely give of themselves, and develops into mutual enhancement.

When two people decide to marry there is an inherent promise and that promise is "I will reveal to you the essence of who you are." One cannot know oneself without the assistance of someone else. Parents are responsible for the development of their children's self–perception. The development of our identity does not stop at the age of twenty–one, but is a life–long process. Who we are is determined by how others view us and whether or not we accept their view. Spouses' perception of each other are of enormous significance. We are least aware of who we are when we are most involved in what we are doing. When we are totally involved in our work, for example, we have the least amount of self-awareness. Often, one partner in a couple will reveal to the other what was previously unknown to him/her. When that partner accepts as true the loving perception of the other it helps the spouse to make a statement to the world of who he/she is. With the insight of the other, one is able to see more clearly—to view the world and put everything into place and perspective: relationships past and present, one's purpose, direction, and very understanding of life. The process of sharing and being accepted, revealing oneself and being happy in the knowledge of what is revealed is what leads to the profound intimacy and unity of a covenant relationship.

The following case illustrates how a husband was a loving and supportive witness to his wife, thus allowing her to claim parts of herself which she could not previously have done:

> Mrs. James was initially seen alone. The presenting problem was poor self esteem. Her husband of fifteen years was invited to the sessions to assist the therapist. Even though Mrs. James had demonstrated that she was a nurturing and competent wife, mother and

friend, she believed herself to be worthless. She rejected positive input from others and minimized her educational and business accomplishments. She believed that she was acting a role which prevented others from really knowing her. She believed that if people understood her inner core they would reject her because they would find her repulsive.

Mrs. James' poor self concept was clearly related to her childhood. She had been born out of wedlock and had never known her father. Her earliest recollections were ones of having been sexually and physically abused, often by her mother's lovers and by family members. She was also responsible for raising four younger stepsiblings whom her mother had neglected. The only nurturing relationship she can remember was one with her grandmother.

Through various therapeutic interventions, Mrs. James was able to recognize the etiology of her poor self esteem, to relinquish the negative impact her early childhood experiences had on her development, and to claim positive attributes herself. However, the key factor in Mrs. J's development of autonomy was the support given her by her husband. He was able to recognize the many admirable qualities she possessed. He cited many examples of her demonstrations of love and unselfishness in the years of their marriage. He was also able to help her to see how she validated him and had helped him to grow.

Helping one's partner to grow and develop can be accomplished at a very profound level, as is demonstrated in this case. But it can also be present in the small challenges of everyday living. Loving partners do this with intuitive gestures of validation and by the active support of the aspirations, needs and activities of the loved one.

There must be stipulations in marriage as the partners have different understanding of what is important, and have different expectations and different needs. In a covenant marriage the first stipulation is faithfulness. Each should always speak in loving truth. Not speaking this truth will inevitably lead to distrust, suspicion and distancing. With a loving truthful discourse always intact, differences can be addressed and there is in place a mechanism to insure that the we psyche in such relationships will be not only in place, but will be harmonious and mutually enhancing.

It is not always an easy thing to speak the truth lovingly. It requires that the partners be autonomous and have in place a good amount of dignity. It also requires that the partners have an awareness of their own feelings and an ability to communicate the feelings. The case of Mr. and Mrs. Katz illustrates how couples can have difficulty if they do not have these abilities, even though they do experience love for one another.

> Mr. and Mrs. Katz were seen in therapy because of an expressed lack of communication. The couple was asked to discuss a problem which distanced them. Mr. Katz complained that his wife refused to go camping with him. She hated sleeping on the ground being in the cold, and insects. In watching the couple interact, Mr. Katz presented himself in a demanding and angry manner. He would shout "Damn it! You never want to try anything that don't come with the comforts of life!" or "What's the matter with you, don't you want any adventure in your life?" Such statements only angered Mrs. Katz and furthered her resolve not to go camping.
>
> When I explored Mr. Katz' feelings about why he wanted his wife to go with him, he indicated that he missed her on these trips, he felt lonely without her and he wished that she could enjoy the beauty of the outdoors with him. He was asked to tell her these feelings and thoughts. In so doing, he invited her to be attentive to him, rather than demanding of her compliance. She was then free to accept or refuse his invitation. Mrs. Katz was moved by his reasons and reacted sensitively. She told him that she appreciated his thoughtfulness and was sad that she could not do as he wished. Although she still refused to go, the sadness and tenderness they experienced bonded them closer as a couple.

Couples cannot always come to agreement on issues. If however, they communicate in a truthful, loving way, as demonstrated above, they can learn to better accept differences.

Speaking in loving truth means speaking supportively rather than in criticism. Mr. G., for example, was upset because his wife had too much to drink at a party the previous night and had acted rudely. He indicated in a supportive way that because he knew she would not ordinarily behave in a way that might alienate people from her, he was concerned about her. Mr. G. in addressing the problem, allowed his wife to recognize that he knew her and that he was concerned about her. This in turn invited rather than demanded an appreciative response.

Further, there needs to be clearly defined evidence that a covenant relationship exists—a sign that is very specific and easily recognized. That sign is the sacrifice a spouse offers to enhance the well-being of his/her partner. A true manifestation of love and one of the cornerstones of a covenant relationship is giving of oneself for the sake of the other—demanding nothing in return but instead hoping the sacrifice makes the partner happy, and validates the essence of the other. Love is giving. The sacrifice offered is a gift—a gift of oneself to the other and a gift of love. O. Henry describes this kind of sacrifice as "generosity added to love." His short story, *The Gift of the Magi,* illustrates an ideal act of love. In the famous tale, Della and Jim are in love and in debt. It is almost Christmas and each wants to give the other a gift. This couple possesses two things about which they are inordinately proud—her luxurious knee-length hair and his grandfather's only legacy—an ornate gold watch. Della sells her hair to buy Jim a platinum watch fob chain and Jim sells the watch to buy Della a set of jeweled tortoise-shelled combs. The gift is love on so grand a scale that O. Henry speculates that the Wise Men—the Magi—would have brought such a gift to the Babe in the manger. He concludes the story:

> ". . . and here I have lamely related to you the uneventful chronicle of two foolish children in a flat who most unwisely sacrificed for each other the greatest treasures of their house. But in a last word to the wise of these days—let it be said that of all who give gifts these two were the wisest. All who give and receive gifts such as they are the wisest. Everywhere they are the wisest. They are the Magi." [4]

In a covenant relationship, the desire to meet the needs of ones partner before meeting ones own needs is manifested from the start. At the beginning of the relationship, for example, one will ask where the partner would like to go to dinner rather than insist on a specific place. I have observed in my practice that the need for and desire to give in a relationship is recognized by most couples. When I ask couples "What is love to you?" they will invariably make a statement such as "giving to my spouse," "giving up my needs for my partner," or "putting my spouse first." I believe that the desire to give to a loved one is intrinsic to and is a requirement of intimacy. Offering a loving sacrifice can be demonstrated on a daily basis in small ways, such as joyfully entering into the spouse's plans for the evening even if the partner would have preferred something else. It can also be demonstrated on a grander scale—giving up one's job and moving away from family and friends so that a professional or business goal can be realized. However it is manifested, the act of giving sets in motion and highlights a number of marital dynamics and issues essential to an enhancing relationship.

First, the making of loving sacrifices establishes a relationship in which couples continually take into consideration the feelings, needs and beliefs of the other, leading to a freeing rather than confining interactional or transactional processes. This process allows for the flexibility in problem solving which is required for spouses to adapt and/or accommodate to the major differences they bring into the relationship. Areas of difference include: beliefs, habits, values, personality traits, religion, relationship expectations, life goals, money management, desire for and needs of children and relationships with extended family. In every relationship adaptation and/or accommodation can and will be met to some degree with a "bargaining process." In other words, couples will problem solve differences by finding something that is either mutually acceptable or trading—i.e., we will do it this way your time and my way next time. Although necessary, this latter process is not nearly as enhancing to the relationship as problem solving by giving out of love.

Second, by making loving sacrifices, a relationship is perpetuated which allows for true acceptance of differences, thus encouraging each partner to be who he/she can be in the world. In relationships where there are no loving sacrifices, spouses often believe that they accept differences when in fact they have accommodated, and sometimes only begrudgingly accommodated. In such relationships resentment often builds because of the accommodation, which leads to emotional distancing.

Third, the giving of a loving sacrifice will acknowledge to the receiver that his/her thoughts, feelings and beliefs are being taken into consideration and validated. This creates feelings of warmth, kindness and generosity in the receiver, which in turn instills the desire to want to give back, not out of guilt or obligation, but out of loving feelings. Thus a process of mutual giving is established, often leading to spouses trying to out give one another. For example, a couple is arguing about where to go on vacation—each having a different destination of choice. After hearing and validating how important it is for his wife to visit her family, the husband wanted to support her. Moved by her love and understanding she acknowledged to him how important it was for him to take his dream vacation and began indicating that perhaps they should vacation where he originally wished to go.

Fourth, the giving of a loving sacrifice provides to the receiver tangible evidence that he/she is loved. Such evidence makes the receiver feel special, and will help each person feel safe and united.

Fifth, the giving of a loving sacrifice facilitates trust in a relationship. Recognizing the tangible evidence that one is loved, a person will feel safe in being him/her self and creates an atmosphere in which spouses feel they are able to share their deepest, most sensitive thoughts, feelings and insecurities. When profound trust has been established, spouses know that what is being said can be taken at face value. Each trusts that the other is always acting in good faith and toward a goal of enhancement of the partner.

Finally, in the giving of a loving sacrifice, the giver loses something and in some instances will suffer from the loss. For example, a spouse might experience tremendous sadness and loss at not being near his/her family because of a move made for the spouse's professional advancement. However, at a deeper level, the spouse who made the sacrifice loses nothing for he/she is also enhanced, as one of the most wonderful feelings one can have is the feeling of goodness from having sacrificed out of feelings of love. "It is better to give than to receive" is the cliche— I would regard it "To give is to receive."

The evidence of love given by the loving sacrifice insures that "I trust that you will always act in my best interest." With this trust, I can then assume that you will be faithful, honest and loving. I will reveal to you in loving way your identity and we will both flourish in an atmosphere where we can both delight in each other as we help each other achieve our full human potential. I will delight in sharing with you a life of happiness and fulfillment.

The "silver cord" which binds a covenant relationship is the reciprocity which must exist in the relationship. Both spouses should be ready to share a life of love and be willing to put the essence of who they are and what they will become at stake. Each spouse should wish to help the other to a better understanding of true self and each must truly enjoy knowing the other. Both should be faithful and speak the truth in loving consideration of each other. Finally, both should be willing to make loving sacrifices. There cannot be a covenant relationship without these conditions being reciprocated.

A covenant relationship allows for a positive "we psyche" to grow while at the same time it facilitates autonomy. First, in a covenant relationship partners agree to marry because of loving feelings which draw them together so that feelings of "we-ness" or completion are experienced. This is manifested by couples wanting to do things together rather than alone, wanting to share happy and important moments, wanting to unify their love by having children and by expressions such as "I feel empty without you." At the same time, the partner is loved for the qualities that are evidence and there is no demand from either for change. This allows for autonomy.

Second, autonomy is facilitated in a covenant relationship when, with the aid of his/her partner, a spouse learns more about him/herself. The more I know about myself, the more I can manifest those qualities and characteristics. I will never be a great artist, for example, without a canvas and without paint. Someone has to show me where to get these things. Thus, as I learn more about myself, I learn more about ways I can enhance my spouse's happiness.

Third, in being faithful and in speaking the truth, I am being myself by revealing to my partner my honest thoughts, feelings, beliefs and values. In so doing, a trust is created which allows us to resolve or accept differences and to feel safe with one another. Such an atmosphere facilitates closeness and intimacy.

Finally, with each partner making loving sacrifices, spouses know they are loved, thus once again grow toward closeness and autonomy. In the offering and acceptance of a relationship based on loving sacrifice spouses feel truly bonded. Autonomy is maintained concurrently as each is motivated for loving concern in nurturing the growth and well-being of the other.

In summary, a covenant relationship reinforces individual freedom and facilitates flexibility so that each spouse is encouraged to enjoy life in a way which is satisfactory and which allows, indeed encourages, maximum fulfillment as a human being. A covenant relationship amplifies loving feelings and establishes a marriage based on profound trust, friendship and respect. This does not mean that the marriage will be free from conflict, misunderstandings or deep emotional pain. But in the presence of profound trust and love, even these experiences will bring the couple to a deeper level of understanding and closeness. Within such a marriage, intimacy can be shared, feelings of completeness can be experienced, and the fusion of emotional energy will serve to expand the relationship out into the world.

In developing confidence within ourselves, we begin to relate to the world differently. We might become more social, risk more experiences, try on a new philosophy. We might become more supportive of others, or more assertive in our relationships. We benefit not only in our relationship, but the world around us.

A covenant marital relationship represents a certain kind of interconnectedness, however, it does not assume that a satisfactory relationship cannot be achieved short of this ideal. The less a relationship is based on reasons other than love—such reasons as selfishness, insecurity, dependency, the more the marriage will stifle autonomy and nurture a rigid, controlling relationship. Such relationships can be bonded—in fact some are glued so tightly together the autonomous selves can never be extricated.

4

AUTONOMY
AND
DIGNITY

OFTEN, AUTONOMY IS INTERPRETED as either physical separation or emotional unconnectedness. In fact, one can be physically separated yet have very little autonomy and, conversely, live with one's spouse and family and have a great deal of autonomy. Individuals are always influenced by other relationships, the most significant ones being the closest.

Therefore, the issue is never one of not being influenced by other relationships. The issue is always—under what circumstances and to what degree am I controlling these influences. I believe the autonomous person to be one who, while they may or may not recognize past or current influences, responds to these influences out of feelings of security rather than insecurity.

Autonomy then, is a state of being in which I have integrated, in a positive way, all my past experiences—even damaging ones—and I have now, sometimes subconsciously, chosen out of these experiences those values and beliefs that I accept—that are my own, that are enhancing to me and my relationship with the world.

Who are we? Lord Byron said, "I live not in myself but I become a portion of that around me." Many years ago, in conducting a workshop for Asian American health professionals, I informed the audience that I was male, Chinese, married, had two children, was a social worker and of the Roman Catholic faith; that my parents were born in China and were very traditional; that I was one of eight children; that for the first five years of my life I was raised by Black foster parents, and then I grew up in a neighborhood which was 95% Mexican–American. Then I asked, rhetorically, "Which of these roles do you suppose influenced me the most?" This is a question which cannot be answered. We have all been influenced by a variety of experiences which we cannot effectively measure in intensity or affect. However, the successful integration of my life experiences will be a measure of my autonomy.

The key variable in the development of autonomy is the degree to which an individual is able to internalize dignity. The depth of internalization of dignity is influenced both by the amount of love and support a person receives and by the amount of freedom that person is able to exercise.

This author believes that every infant is born with an intrinsic, specifically human dignity which is intact; that birth is miraculous in itself and that there is in every birth the potential for the development of a fully loving human adult. As the infant grows and develops, it is necessary that the incipient quality of dignity be reinforced by nurturing care and loving acts. If enough of the child's inborn dignity has been preserved by such care, this person will internalize the feeling that he/she is a loving and lovable human being and will thus be able to integrate even devastatingly negative experiences in a non-destructive manner.

If parents or guardians do not provide love and nurturing, the child's dignity will be attacked, leading to an alienation of dignity. This deprivation will result in psychological insecurities, many of which will be manifested as feelings of abandonment, the feeling of being unlovable, stupid or unattractive, and/or a fear of physical vulnerability.

As psychological insecurities develop, emotional wounds are created. The earlier the infliction of the psychological pain, the greater the intensity of the pain; the longer the pain is experienced—the deeper the wound. Bandages people use for psychological wounds are: projection, displacement, denial, rationalization, and withdrawal. But bandages never heal a wound and in fact can interfere with its healing, just as defense mechanisms can perpetuate inappropriate, dysfunctional and sometimes destructive coping methods.

The only thing that can heal psychological wounds is for the afflicted to apply the balm of knowledge that he/she is lovable and worthwhile, or to have it applied by a loving other. But the underlying immune system, that is, one's human dignity, must be intact in order for healing to take place. If it is, the human psyche can withstand tremendous injury and still be capable of healing, although the healing process can often be prolonged and painful.

Studies indicate that children who have suffered from tremendous deprivation, emotional and physical pain, or sexual abuse, have been able to integrate even these experiences and go on to develop into healthy happy adults if there was a loving relationship in early childhood which encouraged bonding and allowed the internalization of human dignity to occur. Further, we unconsciously and non–verbally receive and internalize an infinite number of messages, not only from those people with whom we are in contact, but from everything in our environment. Often these messages enhance our dignity without our necessarily being aware of the process. Such messages will help in the process of the development of self-worth. There will be those who will need help in this process, as exemplified in the following case history:

> K., a thirteen-year-old Mexican–American female, was referred to me by her pediatrician because she was exhibiting oppositional behavior which was life threatening. She was diabetic and was not staying on her diet or taking her insulin shots on schedule. Additionally, she was becoming verbally abusive, her grades in school were dropping and she was becoming socially isolated. It was learned that K's maternal grandmother had been her primary caretaker for several months as the child's mother. Mrs. Z. was often in jail on drug charges or unavailable for other reasons.
>
> In the first session, K. was brought by her mother and her mother's lover, Mr. Y. The child was appropriately dressed and groomed. She appeared to me to be warm, sensitive, intelligent, charming and shy. Mrs. Z described K.'s behavior in a genuinely concerned manner. It was evident that although there were some glaring problems with Mrs. Z's care–taking abilities, she loved K. and was troubled by the child's self–destructive behavior. Mr. Y. also showed concern about K.'s welfare. K. would not speak in this atmosphere and so it was decided that she would be seen alone.
>
> In private session with K., it was revealed that she had been subjected to extremely traumatic experiences, especially in the preceding six months. She was being raised in an environment which

included a mother with drug and alcohol addictions, a verbally
abusive part–time father, a battering step–father, sub–standard,
constantly changing housing, threats of abandonment, and she had
recently learned about the kind of permanent treatment she would
need for her recently diagnosed diabetes. K. said that there was no one
she could talk to about her problems but expressed a willingness to try
to talk to her mother at my suggestion.

Given this environment, I find K's behavior understandable. What
was striking is this case was that, in spite of all of this, she had not lost
her dignity. Somewhere, somehow, she had received the message at a
very deep level that she was worthy of love. If given direction and
support there is no doubt in my mind that this she could lead a
successful life. She is in touch with the largely unverbalized feeling of
love and support from her mother, father and her grandmother. It will
take a lot of work with K. and her mother, but I believe that this child
will be capable of making the conscious and unconscious choices necessary to internalize her experiences in a positive way and thus develop a
high degree of autonomy. Treatment with this family will need to focus
upon issues of appropriate nurturance and care as well as upon the
amount of freedom to make age appropriate decisions K. is allowed. As
previously indicated, the ability to manifest freedom has a major influence on the depth to which an individual will be able to internalize
dignity. Our dignity is enhanced when we are free to choose and therefore understand that we have some control over what is to be. Freedom,
then, establishes our dignity and assures dignity in all our choices.

Freedom is generally understood to be the right or privilege to freely
choose. However, the concept of freedom encompasses much more. I
believe that every person has the intrinsic right to be free to manifest
who they truly are to him/herself and to others. When freedom influences others, it is often at the others' expense. For example, a wife might
believe that she has the freedom to stay out all night drinking while her
husband is home worrying. Freedom, therefore, is not simply license to
"do my own thing." Responsibility must accompany freedom. A free
and responsible person takes into consideration the rights of others
while expressing freedom.

Children often believe they have the right to do as they please, i.e., not attend school. Most children do not have the cognitive ability nor psychological and developmental maturity to make appropriate decisions. They do not realize that they are not truly responsible for themselves and are dependent upon their parents. It is their parents who are legally, financially and morally responsible for them. Children want freedom without responsibility. If children are to grow into responsible adults, parents must provide an age-appropriate structure in which the child can make decisions.

In summary, autonomy is a state of being in which an individual has integrated, in a positive way, both positive and negative life experiences and is therefore capable of making mature decisions. The development of autonomy is based on the amount of dignity an individual is able to manifest. The depth of internalization of dignity is influenced by the love and nurturance a person receives and gives, and by the personal freedom felt and expressed. Some individuals are so alienated from their dignity that they have little autonomy and are thus emotionally paralyzed. They believe that they have no freedom to make decisions which will lead them to live fulfilling lives. On the other hand, some are able to achieve a depth of dignity such that their autonomy will remain intact no matter what challenges life presents to them. Nouwen writes about such a person:

> I would like to tell you the story of a middle–aged man whose career was suddenly interrupted by the discovery that he had leukemia, a fatal blood cancer. All his life plans crumbled and all his ways had to change. But slowly he was able to ask himself, "Why did this have to happen to me? What did I do to deserve this fate?" But instead: "What is the promise hidden in this event?" when his rebellion became a new quest, he felt that he could give strength and hope to other cancer patients and, that by facing his condition directly, he could make his pain into a source of healing for others. To this day, this man not only does more for patients than many ministers are able to do, but he also refound his life on a level that he had never known before.[5]

II

Marital
Development

5

STAGES OF MARITAL DEVELOPMENT

THE FIRE

The fire was slow kindling—it was damp wood
Old, and moistened by the earth and rain
Two times I rose to mend it from your side
Stirred the wet sticks and blew the smoldering ends
Then in the clear cold night and clearing of the wood
We two, under the stars, hearts not young
And wet with time's worse rain, forgot the fire.

Until it suddenly was there, each kindled point
Enforcing another—to take us by surprise
A brightness huge and fierce, a living flame,
That sent up sparks to coil among the stars—
Earth's poor matter assaulting the night skies,
A trembling moment of eternity
That was the constellation of our love . . .[6]

Charles G. Bell

THAT WE ARE NOT ALWAYS IN TOUCH WITH our loving feelings does not mean that they do not exist. As the marriage develops feelings will constantly change. I have here defined what I believe to be the stages of marital development which will lead toward a successful relationship. The phases, which are evolutionary but not mutually exclusive are:

1. Enchantment Phase
2. Disenchantment Phase
3. Negotiation Phase
4. Integration Phase
5. Enhancement Phase
6. Covenant Phase

In the "enchantment phase" of the relationship, which is primarily based on feelings, the couple "falls in love." During this phase, the couple catches glimpses of the "covenant relationship." The partners have a sense of autonomy that is related to feeling understood and validated. They become aware of their dignity, an awareness which is manifested in the desire to please the other. In so doing, they express a feeling of goodness from within. Partners often have an awareness of freedom and safety which allows their "playful child" to surface. They wish to be best friends and to share adventures and activities. The activities can be anything—bicycling, sailing or fishing. It does not matter. The being together, enjoying each other's company is what is important. There is that special experiencing of intimacy when the hearts, minds, bodies and spirits of lovers are joined together in a loving relationship.

In the "enchantment phase" couples establish hope that they will have a mutually enhancing future together. The also hope their partner will continue to desire to be attentive to them. The fire burns brightly and the couple feels warmth, understanding and admiration for each other. They might begin noticing small things which are irritable or disappointing but caught up in the feeling of love these things seem trivial. Real potential problem areas are minimized and discounted. Love, after all "conquers all."

After the "enchantment phase," which might last a few months, weeks, or not survive the honeymoon night, couples move on to the "disenchantment phase." Romantic feelings begin to diminish and the individuals begin to exhibit their true behaviors, feelings and attitudes. Cognitive reality begins to return and the fire dims. Suddenly all those non–important issues; step–children problems, money, in–laws, career goals, differences in world–view, loom large and threatening. Consequently, it is during this phase that it is important for couples to be aware that love is more than just "romantic feelings." There are often times during this period when the partners feel far from romantic. The recognition that love is something concrete—a belief and not just "feelings' will allow couples to realistically and objectively appraise the condition of their relationship. It will also reinforce the hope of attaining an enhancing marriage.

During the disenchantment phase some couples begin to feel disappointment, sorrow, or anger. Others begin to question their love or their decision to marry. Still others feel helpless and wonder if they will ever be able to resolve differences or accept characteristics in their partner which they find unattractive. Because of the emotional burden of this phase, couples move quickly to the "negotiation phase."

In the "negotiation phase," couples attempt to resolve their now apparent areas of conflict. During this phase the marriage is tested. This is where the "hard work" begins to build a mutually enhancing relationship. There is a cold chill in the air. Even the most loving and caring people can remain in the "negotiation phase" because they do not know how to avoid the "natural traps" in marriage.

To successfully pass through the "negotiation phase" of marriage, partners must learn to enter into discussions with maturity. Flexibility is required and each spouse must allow the partner the freedom to be different and to hold different opinions. The resolution of problems must be based on mutual satisfaction rather than one partner giving in. There will be times when couples cannot share the same view or come to a mutually agreeable solution to a problem. But differences can be overcome if the partners do not negate the opinions and beliefs of the other, but treat each other's differing opinions with respect.

It is during the "negotiation phase" that the demonstration of love is the most difficult and where it is most needed. What better way to demonstrate love than to be attentive to the needs and wishes of the partner while attempting to resolve potentially divisive issues. If couples can manifest loving gestures by giving of themselves during this phase, the hope that the partner will be faithful is verified, reinforcing the belief that the partner wishes to be a loving witness. This builds assurance that the future will be lovingly shared.

If couples are able to negotiate effectively, they enter into the "integration phase" of the relationship. Here they are able to discuss issues and problems and share ideas in a supportive, mature way. In so doing, they are able to integrate differences, establish harmony and create a peaceful routine in the marriage. The couples have also demonstrated the ability to be attentive to the others' needs and to exhibit mutual respect and trust. There is a greater awareness of the essence of the other and an interaction pattern in which the partners are mutually supportive and encouraging. Autonomy has been maintained and both partners feel the freedom to be themselves.

During the "integration phase" of marriage, many couples become complacent. Basking in the warm glow of the relationship, they believe that this is all that marriage can become. Romantic feelings diminish and partners stop being best friends. They lose sight of why they married in the first place. As a result, both partners develop other areas of interest which sometimes assume paramount importance. In this stage of the relationship the couple might develop a peaceful co-existence, or they might drift emotionally apart.

If the couple continues to put loving effort into their relationship, the marriage will move into the glowing "enhancement phase." Time is set aside for attention to each other. The couple develops a life together which is separate from other relationships. They remain best friends and do such things as travel together, discuss ideas, and plans, listen and learn from each other. Throughout this process, loving feelings continue to develop.

Couples reach the "covenant phase" of the relationship when each experiences the other's love as a constant reality. The relationship is not devoid of conflicts, even severe ones; however a good balance between the autonomy of the spouses and the "we psyche" has been established. Profound trust and respect are present. Spouses are each other's best friends and want their partners to be free to develop private interests. Loving offerings are freely given and each spouse feels joy in contributing to the happiness of the other. The fire burns brightly—the feelings in the "enhancement phase" are not only rekindled, but they are enhanced by the couples' greater understanding of each other, shared experiences, and investment in the dignity of the partner.

In the "covenant phase," spouses recognize that they have established an enhancing relationship, but that it is never complete. They continue to hope for more in the future. Each day offers new adventures, new challenges and new insights into themselves as well as their partners. Couples feel secure in their ability to face any crisis which might arise. Finally, they are secure in that knowledge that their partner is faithful, will be a loving witness and will be with them to share a life of love and happiness.

6

CULTURAL INFLUENCES ON MARITAL EXPECTATION

THERE IS LITTLE PUBLIC AWARENESS of the reasons behind the high divorce rate in this country and thus the public tends to simplify its analysis of the reason couples separate. Emphasis is focused on individual shortcomings or lack of effort on the part of the spouse. Friends of a couple in conflict will say such things as: "If he were less selfish the marriage would have worked," or, "Couples don't try hard enough these days—it's easy just to get up and leave." Although psychological insecurities do have a role in disrupting marital harmony, the causal factors in divorce are numerous and studies indicate that most people do not just walk away from a marriage but will, in fact, spend years trying to make it work even in the face of major problems in the marriage. Additional years are spent delaying the act of divorce even after all hopes for happiness in the relationship are lost.

A lot of us grew up watching *Father Knows Best* and *Ozzie and Harriet* where there is never more than one problem at a time, everyone is reasonable and pretty and cheerful, and nothing ever happens that can't be resolved to everyone's satisfaction in one half hour. Then millions of Americans watched the *Walton* kids listen to their elders and do their chores. We graduate to *Dynasty* and *Dallas* and learned that the things that really count are money and power, selfishness and lust. A relationship is based on superficial possessiveness which is constantly (understandably) threatened by the possibility of another superficial relationship.

Of course we cannot blame the media for crowded divorce courts, but in this age of visual education I think that one can safely say that

42

many people's perceptions of what a marriage ought to be are influenced by superficial notions of what can be expected. The do not know how much more is possible. There is nothing more enhancing than to be loved in an open trusting reciprocal way. A covenant relationship is more than "romantic love." Romantic love is itself a legacy from the days of "courtly love."

COURTLY LOVE

Courtly love is a 12th century concept started by the troubadours of Southern France. This theme states that romantic love must always be tragic, unrequited, irrational, unpredictable, frenzied and necessarily temporary. It is therefore one of the poorest reasons for marriage. Romantic love looks to Eros, while married love is based on Agape, human love. In courtly love, one projects ones fantasy on the other and does not see the other person as a full human being. Robert Johnson, in the book, *We,* holds the opinion that it is our search for a heavenly altered state of consciousness that puts energy into building a fantasy upon the love object, so the love object is truly not seen as person with hopes, ambitions, shortcomings, but rather becomes a manifestation of the projector's vision of what it is to be loved. A lover falls in love with the idea of love rather than the object of his love, and keeping in the tradition of courtly love, sexual fulfillment is to be avoided—the passion of romantic love is fueled by the tension between desire and fulfillment. Courtly love was on a higher plane, a more tortuous plane, a nobler plane. This torture can be seen in the central theme in the legend of *Tristan and Isolde.* Isolde is married to the king and Tristan is one of her loyal knights. Their romantic love is built on the inability of really being together—chance meetings, glances, whispers, all mark the pain of their romantic love. Finally they run off together. In the woods their love quickly dies. Courtly love is necessarily temporary. They return to the king and beg his forgiveness, he forgives them, and no sooner are things in place then they begin to sneak off together again.[7]

The modern view of romantic love; a legacy of courtly love, is that love is tragic, furtive, idealistic, noble and impossible. This is the concept that is at the heart of all our modern "romantic" books, plays and movies. The message we receive is that love is something which exists outside of marriage or precedes it, it is based on an idealization of the beloved and involves intense sexual longings which can never really be fulfilled as there is no permanent commitment. Marriage is viewed as a convenient living arrangement which is peripheral to love or even a ceremony marking the end of romantic love.

All the great and not so great love stories have this requisite formula, i.e., man and woman fall in love but cannot be together and thus the story ends tragically; Romeo and Juliet die together, Anna Karenina jumps in front of a train; Cyrano de Bergerac and Christian both predecease Roxanne; in *Casablanca,* Ilse flies off with a man she does not love while Rick watches her airplane leave in the rain, ennobled in his decision to give her up; and in *Love Story,* Ali McGraw dies a perfectly serene, lovely death while Ryan O'Neal walks off into the snowstorm. In those cases where both partners survive and actually remain together, the story ends before the wedding.

But a careful reading of those really great authors who were not bound by the romantic conventions of their time will affirm that married love was not negated, just not usually directly addressed. Vladimir Nabokov, in his book, *Lectures on Russian Literature,* directs us to read between the lines of what is probably the prototype love story, Anna Karenina.

> "Tolstoy, in a flow of extraordinary imagery depicts and places side by side, in vivid contrast, two loves: the carnal love of the Vronski–Anna couple (struggling amid their richly sensual but spiritually sterile emotions) and on the other hand, Christian love, as Tolstoy termed it, of the Levin–Kitty couple with the riches of sensual nature still there but balanced and harmonious in the pure atmosphere of responsibility, tenderness, truth and family joys."[8]

In a "covenant relationship," romantic feelings have room to expand and grow. There is some idealization of the beloved, but as each partner becomes what the other imagines him/her to be the idealization is perpetuated by changes which are constantly occurring and fueling the loving feelings and passions of the relationship. The partner is seen as real; human and yet possessed of those qualities which inspire sacrifice and gratitude. The reciprocity and permanence of the marriage provide a strong and safe structure on which the relationship can continue to build.

In a covenant relationship the emphasis is on the "we" and not on the "I." It is very American to idealize the individual. This country was founded on the ideal of independence and our folk heroes are strong, capable and self–reliant. Our democratic spirit fosters Horatio Alger qualities—clear independent vision, standing alone and strong—not dependent on anyone or anything, never looking for support, even from the government. We teach our children that they must be "individuals," must become their own "persons." We direct children toward goals of personal achievement. Self–help books emphasize "self–actualization" and encourage a belief that we are responsible only for ourselves. People come away with ideas that lead them to make such statements as: "If she feels hurt by what I said, that is her problem." The emphasis on the "I" is consistent with the American experience.

We must differentiate, however, between what might be sound politically and what is necessary in human relationships. I do not believe that it is psychologically sound to emphasize the "I" and the concept of "individuation." Most people, even mental health professionals, understand "individuation" as "separation." This "separation" turns into a quest for "self-fulfillment" which, when no other directions are given, will end with self–centeredness. When I ask couples why they married, I often find they will respond with such answers as: "I married him/her because I believed that he/she could meet my needs." I seldom hear such sentiments as "I wanted to make him happy and to meet his/her needs." It is unrealistic to expect that a person who is raised with all the energy on the "I" will change that orientation simply because of marriage. The value will surface as conflict as each spouse works toward the goal of self–satisfaction. Stressing the "I" gives us the illusion that the ideal state is one of unconnectedness—a state which is neither easy to achieve nor even desirable. We all need emotional connectedness, especially the feeling of being loved and wanted and we all fear being abandoned and alone. The fact is that we are social beings, always involved in social intercourse and always responsible to and for different people in a variety of circumstances.

Most importantly, our lives are part of an evolutionary process whereby we are always growing, adapting and changing—incorporating into our beings all we experience in life. Life, then, is a process of integration, not separation. In truly accepting ourselves we must integrate, in a positive way, all our experiences, especially those occurring in primary relationships. The more this is accomplished, the more autonomous we will become.

It is necessary that, in a covenant relationship, there is a recognition and emphasis on our common humanity and of the beautiful and meaningful qualities we are able to experience in each other. Awareness of our human dignity and specialness will encourage a relationship which enhances our ability to rejoice in and encourage others' goodness. Our society focuses us away from this core of goodness and projects us into a world of materialism, objectification of human beings, and a concept of built–in obsolescence. This is a throw–away culture. It is easy to dispose of things that don't work. This is easier than fixing them. This concept can easily extend to relationships. We objectify people, ignoring the substance and constantly working on renovating the facade. More and more of us live in cities, walking on cement and living life in the "fast lane." As we detach from nature, we tend to lose sight of our connection to nature and to humanity. We provide each other with material possession and become indifferent to real needs. It is not uncommon to hear a husband say, "I brought her everything she wanted, but she was never satisfied."

The pressures of a rapidly changing society also work against the development of a covenant relationship. We are constantly confronted with change: advancements in science, technology and medicine; changes in political and economic realities; changes in the perceptions of the roles of men and women. It is change, rather than stability, which is the norm. It is now rare for a child to grow up in the same house or even in the same neighborhood. There are problems connected with child care and with adequate housing. The problems of constant uprooting brings with it the breakdown of the extended family support system. Given all the adjustments couples must make, even in the best of circumstances, societal pressure can be overwhelming.

7

CAUSES
OF
CONFLICT

ALTHOUGH SOCIAL FACTORS INFLUENCE expectations for marriage, couples come to therapy with specific and unique problems. When asked what are the causal factors for problems in the marriage, the majority of people will indicate that communication is a problem; the other partner is selfish; they are different and cannot adapt to each other; or they cannot come together on child rearing views or practices.

These are true problems, but the real underlying causes for conflict are more profound. They can generally be classified into the following five categories:

1. Problematic Beginnings
2. Adjustment Problems
3. Individual Insecurities
4. Family Developmental Problems
5. Situational Problems

These categories were established to assist both the marital therapist and his/her clients to conceptualize the etiology for the marital discord. These categories are broad enough to include the range of specific problems brought into therapy. Specific couples might have problems from a combination of categories.

A. PROBLEMATIC BEGINNINGS

Many couples marry for the wrong reasons and thus structure their future on a weak foundation. Instead of deciding to marry to fulfill a mature love, such couples marry out of insecurities, dependency needs or coercion. These couples do not come to the marital event autonomously, nor freely seeking union for its own sake. They have no sense of putting their destiny at stake or allowing their partners to influence the essence of their being. The circumstances of the decision to marry provide the foundation for and affect the development and eventual outcome of the marriage. The marriage would ideally begin with the spouses having strong, loving feelings for one another and choosing to be together because of those feelings. Without this foundation, it is highly unlikely that the couple will achieve happiness and fulfillment in their marriage. Yet many couples do not marry out of strong feelings of love.

Marrying for the wrong reasons is an affront to the partner's dignity. The partner is viewed as an object, the purpose of which is to meet specific needs. Unfaithfulness (in its larger sense, that is betrayal of trust) is implied from the beginning as there is no manifestation of a will to speak with loving truth. The ability for the partners to be loving witnesses is lost and the partner is not asked to share a life of love and happiness, but instead a life of shared dependency. It is selfishness, rather than loving sacrifice which is demonstrated. In short, the partner is asked to participate in a relationship which promises a life of conflict, confusion and despair.

In order to achieve success, a marriage must be based on a foundation of mutual love. The substance of that foundation is two mature loving individuals hoping to make one another happy. Marriage for reasons other than mature love can be quite compelling. After the marriage, the partners quickly recognize that without this substantive love, the initial reason for marrying loses its power. Partners begin to see that they have an inherent need to be accepted and validated for themselves. They begin to feel the need for personal autonomy and their desire to have a best friend whom they can respect and with whom they can share warmth and nurturance. As a result, during the negotiation phase of the relationship, the partners begin to expect and then to demand acceptance as the fear develops that their partner is not being attentive to them. Loving attentiveness was not, after all, part of the original marital agreement, just something that was somehow expected. Thus the relationship develops toward one of control, criticism and emotional distancing.

Here are some examples of problematic situations which push people into marriages which often end unsuccessfully.

Expectant Parenthood

Some men decide to marry because they feel guilty for having made their partner pregnant. They also feel responsible for providing a family for the expectant baby. Some women marry because they are pregnant and any other option for the future is unacceptable to them. Some marry because of parental pressure. Even if the couple have loving feelings for one another, this kind of marriage creates special problems as the couple has no opportunity to adapt to each other before they take on all the new problems connected with being parents.

In one such relationship that was described to me by a client, the woman was trying to end the relationship when she discovered that she was pregnant. She married her lover because she thought he would be a good father (which he was) but also because she felt that if she had the baby alone he would try to get joint custody. Her religion prohibited abortion. He loved her and tried to change to meet her expectations. They tried for seven years to make the marriage work and they had another child. The marriage ended in an amiable divorce. Interestingly, the wife encouraged the husband to take custody of the children.

Running Away From Home

It is not uncommon for someone to marry because pressures at home have become unbearable. At no level does such a person recognize that physical separation does not equal autonomy and that unresolved dependency needs and adequate coping mechanisms will be carried into the marital relationship. Consequently the marriage will begin with a foundation of emotional interdependency which is at first interpreted as love. Many such couples find that parents do not let go that easily and these marriages are often complicated by intrusive meddling from the parents of the spouse that married just to escape such pressures.

A client of mine indicated that she had always been the one in charge of four younger siblings while her mother worked. This "parental child" stated that she did not resent the responsibilities, but became tired of the burdens and restrictions of her role. At nineteen she married her long time boyfriend "just to get out of the house." Her caretaking responsibilities continued, first with her husband, and later when they had a child. After five years of marriage, she changed and began to make demands of her husband who would not or could not meet them. The conflict has grown to the point where she now wishes to end the marriage. In leaving home in the way she chose, little autonomy was established. Instead of growing up and thus outgrowing her family of origin, she grew up and thus outgrew her marriage.

Getting Even With Parents

There are people who marry to deliberately hurt a parent or parents or to prove to the parents that he/she can make an independent adult decision. They would then set out to choose someone whose chief endearing attraction is that the person has just the quality or background that the parent has shown the most antipathy toward. This is marriage out of righteous indignation and as the partner was chosen as a weapon to throw at a parent it is unlikely that real loving feelings will develop.

There is the case of J., a white, middle class liberal, who came of age in the sixties. Her father was a narrow-minded bigot with a special hatred for Jews, Blacks and Hispanics. When she was eighteen, she married a young Jewish musician, S., converted to Judaism and had a huge Jewish wedding which her father refused to attend. Her husband did his best to please the father and after many months the father reluctantly accepted him. Soon after, J. and S. developed a conflictual relationship and they divorced within the year. Six months after the divorce J. married a Black accountant, R., a marriage the father never did accept. This marriage worked for about two years, or until R. began to pressure J. into having a family.

Gentle Force

Some people feel pressured into marriage. In a recent case, for example, the husband indicated that he thought he loved his wife when they married, however he was ambivalent about the marriage because he was not certain of his love and because they constantly argued as a result of her excessive jealousy. His wife admitted that she was "insanely" jealous even before their relationship. However they had been living together for six months and that should have been enough time for him to decide what he truly felt. At some level, she must have been afraid that he would leave the relationship. As is predictable in such cases, the arguing continued and the husband built up resentment for what he felt was a position of having been forced into the marriage. So this is a marriage that began with fear on the part of one partner and ambivalence on the part of the other combining to produce profound distrust on both sides, hardly a strong foundation for a lasting loving relationship.

Sense of Duty

There are people who marry out of obligation. A husband once explained to me that he and his wife had been steadily dating for three years prior to their marriage. He stated that his wife was a virgin prior to their relationship and she had consented to make love with him in anticipation of his readiness to marry her. He no longer felt loving feelings toward her but he feared her hurt and his guilt should he not marry her. He married her in the hope that his feelings would change. They never did, and the couple never became very close, but they were able to maintain a peaceful relationship. Disagreements and arguments started to surface after the birth of their first child. Having children is a real test of the strength of a marriage. This marriage was vulnerable from the start, as the reciprocity of feeling required for a fulfilling relationship was never there.

Financial Investment

Some people view marriage as a business deal. Often the partner who is providing the financial security understands that this was the real reason for the marriage but has the hope that his/her partner's feelings will develop into love. The marriage began with self–centeredness on one side and self–delusion on the other and can rarely grow beyond the emotional level of the business arrangement that it started out to be.

But even in these cases there is some expectation for tenderness and nurturing feelings. I had a client who was complaining that her husband never gave her anything but things and that she resented his recent gift of a pair of expensive earrings. He didn't believe her—he thought he could buy her love. I suggested that as a sign that he was mistaken she could sell the earrings and give the money to charity. She could not do this. She could allow herself to fall back into the business aspect of the marriage but there was less of an investment in feeling.

Teen Love

Statistics tell us that the large majority of teenage marriages will fail. Marriage is an adult relationship and few teenagers have the maturity and knowledge of the world that is required. Adolescents, simply because they are adolescents, cannot, except in very remarkable cases, have matured to the level of being able to give in a relationship. Adolescents are usually appropriately self–centered and are struggling to develop an awareness of themselves and an identity apart from their families. They are still emotionally and often financially dependent on their parents. Working with teenagers is difficult as they have no aware-ness of what it is to be an adult—they simply have not lived long enough.

I will never forget the case of a seventeen-year-old girl who was insisting that she was old enough to marry her eighteen-year-old boyfriend. Her mother tried to explain the problems she could expect but the girl was not receptive to any of it. At the end of the session the girl decided that she would indeed marry her boyfriend. She then turned to her mother and in a child–like voice asked for her five dollar allowance so she and her boyfriend could have gas for his car.

Time is Running Out

Many people still operate out of historically recent convention that it is necessary for a woman to find a good (not necessarily loving) husband, get married young and find fulfillment being a good wife and mother. After about the age of about twenty-three it was probably too late to attract a man and one was doomed to live in a rooming house with a lot of cats. Even today many women have a fear of missing an opportunity and will marry just to escape "spinsterhood." This attitude is exemplified by the young woman in the following interview who was asked why she married her husband. She states:

> "My perception was that I finally found somebody to marry (she puts her hands in the air and indicates quotes) and that I was twenty-four and that time was running out. And he had a lot of good qualities that I like about him. I also realized that a lot of things were in conflict, but I went through with the marriage anyway. . . ."

In this case, and in many like it, the marriage began, not with love, but with insecurity and fear and the spouse was selected on self-centeredness, not on wanting to meet her husband's needs, perhaps not even being aware that he might have had some.

No One Will Ever Marry Me

Some people have so little self–esteem that they believe that they are so undesirable or unlovable that they must settle for anyone. They feel that companionship would be enough. One client said to me, ". . . at my age, I'll take anyone I can get." Many older divorced women feel that in this youth-oriented society, chance for remarriage is slim. Unfortunately, most couples who marry for fear of not finding anyone else discover that being in a loveless relationship has its own problems and being alone had had its own rewards.

Love At First Sight

Often, couples will marry without taking time to know each other. One client told me that she had known her husband for two years before she married him, but because he had overseas duty in the service they had really only been together for four weeks. It was not long after they married that they realized that they were not in love. This was forty-five years ago, when divorce was not considered a respectable option and wartime romance and marriage were elevated to an ideal. A "Dear John" letter was not the only kind of wartime casualty of the heart —so were some of the unhappy long term marriages that developed out of that chaotic time. There are always couples who get caught up in the whirlwind of passionate love and marry within a week of meeting. The early romantic phase over–rides any practical considerations. It is only after knowing each other over a period of time that couples can assess whether an enhancing relationship is possible. It is difficult to end a short romantic relationship but truly painful to end any marriage, even one where the couple never really knew each other at all. Once married—the goal is to make it work in the hope that things will change. Social, religious and family pressures help keep the relationship together.

Such marriages can last decades even if the relationship decays to the level of one described to me by a client who when asked about his feelings toward his wife of forty years said, "I'm too old to consider divorce now, but I hate C. so much I hope that she dies first so I can collect on her life insurance!"

Marriage on the Rebound

Statistics indicate that the large majority of people will remarry within two years following a divorce. These people believe that they will find happiness in a new marriage either because they have learned from their mistakes or they have at last met someone who is capable of meeting their needs. But statistics show that the divorce rate in second marriages is significantly higher than in first. Most people do not allow time to mourn the loss of the first relationship. Because of the tremendous pain present in a conflictual relationship, particularly when separation is imminent, the majority of people will become involved in another relationship during the marriage or just after it ends. There was, for example, the client who came to see me because he was ambivalent about his marriage of fifteen years. When divorce became inevitable for him, we discussed the importance of his not becoming involved in another relationship before he mourned the loss of the marriage. He recognized that need, but was soon involved in a relationship where he thought he was in love—and then another one—until he realized that he really did need to be alone to mourn his marriage.

Unless time passes, people do not resolve within themselves the conflicts and insecurities which created the atmosphere for the divorce. Without mourning the loss of the first marriage, it will be difficult to determine how much of the new relationship is based on love and how much on dependency needs. In any case, unresolved issues from the first marriage will surface during the second, "I don't always do that—your first wife did!"—making the relationship a high risk venture.

Make Me a Match

The practice of arranged marriages still occurs in some cultures in American and is common practice in many countries. Such marriages are not founded on love, but rather traditional values and beliefs. Roles and functions are usually very clear and satisfaction is based on their proper fulfillment. If, however, the value system of either spouse changes, and the subculture influencing the relationship is no longer supportive, conflict could arise. Often, in such cases, women wish more equality in decision making and more attention to their needs. But there is an attitude of a "duty to love" which can lead to a secure and peaceful marriage. M., a woman from Bombay, speaks of her marriage:

> When I was an engaged child, my sister took me to a big house and pointed to an ugly and mean looking boy and said, "That is D. whom you must marry." They tricked me and I was very sad but I knew the boy came from a good family and was going to have a wonderful education and that I could be a good wife and mother and daughter–in–law. But when my wedding came, I saw it was a different boy and kind, and handsome too, and so it would be easier to love him. But it was terrible to be in my mother–in–law's kitchen and she was mean so I went with D. to help him while he studied to be a doctor at a great school in America. It was terrible those years

because he did not respect me when he saw American ladies and was ashamed of my ideas. But we came back to India and now we have a wonderful life—two sons and a house and garden and I am mistress of my home and a good wife and D. is important in the community but sometimes I think that I must be happier than I am.

In summary, in most instances, marriages which began under poor conditions are due to insecurities on the part of one or both partners. More important however, is that such marriages generally begin with at least one of the partners not having loving feelings for the other. Insecurity, coupled with the absence of love, diminishes the possibility of spouses relating in a giving, supportive, enhancing and nurturing manner. Thus both spouses will feel unfulfilled.

B. ADJUSTMENT PROBLEMS

In order to strengthen the foundation of their experience of a loving relationship, spouses must quickly and appropriately adjust from a single lifestyle to a two person alliance during the bargaining phase of marital development. This will require love, autonomy, dignity and the allowance of freedom. Unfortunately many couples are not able to effectively make this transition. In addition to the factor of psychological insecurity, there are three other primary reasons why, in this writer's opinion, couples cannot make the marital adjustment. First, as a society we have not been able to move from the concepts which define a successful traditional marriage to a definition of an enhancing modern marriage. Consequently, couples only vaguely understand what they want from the relationship and what is required of them if it is to succeed. Secondly, couples will inadvertently fall into natural traps which lead to conflict and for some the beginning of the negative spiral. Finally, many couples do not have adequate communication skills.

Historically, marriage was based on traditional values and its purpose was clearly defined by religious or cultural norms. Role and function were clear and each person knew his or her purpose in the family and community. In Chinese society, for example, the family was governed for centuries by the Confucian doctrine which declared:

> Justice between father and son; prudent reserve between husband and wife; respect between elder brother and younger brother; sincerity between elders and juniors; and loyalty between rule and minister.[9]

In many traditional societies marriage was defined by strong religious and cultural norms and these concepts were integrated into this country as people from different cultures immigrated to America. The purpose of marriage was the creation of a family. Large families were necessary to carry on a family name, provide help with domestic chores, retain ownership of property and/or assist the family in earning a living.

Modern union is based on romantic love and the hope of fulfillment or the romantic dream in marriage. But there are no fully defined roles and even the limited roles of twenty years ago (wife/mother–husband/provider) are changing. In contrast to traditional unions, our models are based on the democratic principles of "equal rights" and each spouse is expected to define his/her role in the relationship. Every situation is unique as each partner brings idiosyncratic characteristics and expectations into the marriage. Not only must couples negotiate these differences, they must define for themselves the concept of a "good marriage." Marital enrichment workshops, marriage encounters, pre–marital counseling and marital "cookbooks" are efforts to assist couples in meeting these needs, but these programs do not reach the majority of couples and even if they did, the effectiveness of such methods is questionable.

In the process of resolving differences, couples will perceive unaddressed issues and behave in a way which feels good and is natural. However, in some cases, doing what "feels good" is a trap which will result in conflictual interaction, feelings of rejection, and emotional distancing. Natural marital traps include seeing conflict as necessarily damaging rather than possibly enhancing, believing that couples ought to feel and behave in tandem, believing one's own reality to be always objective and one's spouse's reality to be subjective, involving others in marital conflict, and attempting to rescue one's spouse from emotional pain.

In truth, differences are not by definition bad, they are just differences. Often the freshness of new perceptions and ideas can be a positive force in a marriage. As each person is unique in the world each will bring into the marriage a different set of values, beliefs, behaviors and interests. Differences do not separate couples, it is the inability to accept and integrate differences which causes disharmony.

Insecurities, lack of self–knowledge, and ethnocentrism are some of the things which make a new idea or perspective seem frightening or wrong. But if differences are looked upon as something added to the relationship, people can grow together in new directions. In a covenant relationship, if one partner gets great pleasure from something, for example, the theater, the other might well grow to love it too, first out of a wish to share the experience with the beloved—but later out of a genuine discovery that the theater can be exciting. A rigid wife can teach structure to a receptive, impulsive husband and an impulsive husband can teach a receptive, rigid wife the joys of spontaneity. There is a Yin/Yan wholeness in being able to trust the unique qualities of the other.

There is a natural tendency to desire that one's partner be a clone of oneself. This is the feeling that my partner must think, act, react, behave, even vote, exactly like me. In attempting to force a partner to become a mirror image of themselves, spouses will attempt to control behaviors, attitudes, feelings and sometimes even thoughts. A partner in such a relationship makes such statements as: "You shouldn't feel that way," "You can't really believe that," or "Where did you get such a dumb idea?" In such a situation I feel invalidated or rejected for daring to display an individual thought, behavior or idea. My autonomy is stifled and resentment begins to build. The battle lines are drawn. I will defend my position and thus discount you. The conflict then escalates.

In a mature relationship there is an honest effort to try to understand and to accept differences. Partners will discuss dissenting issues to try to learn the reasons for the behavior shown or the opinion held. In so doing, the partner is invited, not commanded, to change—with the understanding that even if change is not possible, the relationship will accommodate the differences. There is an understanding on both parts of subjective reality and a recognition that the partner is a person capable of interpreting the world with his/her own intellect. Following is a case example of the kind of "my reality must be your reality? Thinking which becomes a set-up for misunderstanding:

> Mrs. R. insisted that she loved her husband but that he did not recognize her constant attempts to please him. Mr. R. did not accept his wife's protestations of love, but said that she was instead only meeting her own needs. Mr. R. related an incident which he said was typical of Mrs. R's displays of devotion. His wife had offered to make him a sandwich. He politely refused, as it had been his experience that his wife made him a sandwich according to her tastes, not his. Mrs. R. insisted on making the sandwich and she did, her way. He became angry (having many times expressed just how he liked his sandwich made). She insisted that this was an example of his not accepting her efforts to please him.

In this case example, Mrs. R. was saying—"accept my love in the way that I choose to express it." When rejected for her efforts, Mrs. R. would become hurt and then angry. She really believed that she was trying to meet her husband's needs. Objectively, however, she was just alienating him further.

Each spouse must be certain that the message given is the message received. A clear interpretation of the message is what will lead to mature discussion of problems.

It is natural for couples to wish to call in a "witness" or "judge" to mediate their conflicts. Often the therapist is cast in this role. Bowen describes why this pattern of "triangulation" occurs:

> The theory states that the triangle, a three-person emotional configuration, is the molecule or the basic building block of any emotional system. A two person system may be stable, as long as it is calm, but when anxiety increases, it immediately involves the most vulnerable other person to become a triangle. When tension is too great for the threesome, it involves others to become a series of inter-locking triangles.[10]

Triangulating a third person in a disagreement is helpful when both partners are receptive to such a tactic. In many instances however, the process facilitates more triangulation and the intensity of the conflict will be played out on a bigger stage and on a grander scale. Often, when someone is called as a "witness," the partner who is "testified against" feels outnumbered, discounted and invalidated. In severely dysfunctional relationships one partner will build a careful "case for the prosecution" the other will present a "case for the defense" leading to a "countersuit." With trust gone, and such dedication to gathering evidence, the marriage might well end up in a real courtroom.

Couples should avoid pleading a special interest case. They must be led to conceptualize their working relationship as a partnership—a holding company which must handle a variety of complex problems. They might well disagree about procedure, but the goal should be to combine their efforts to build the best presentation possible. The purpose is not to out–wit competition or dominate the marketplace of the other. They must learn that they are on the same side.

When one is in emotional pain because of a specific problem, there is an instinctive tendency for the partner to try to take away the pain. This is done both in advice giving and a desire to take on and thus solve the problem. This loving instinct can be dysfunctional, as illustrated in the following case:

> Mr. and Mrs. K had a strong caring relationship but they chose to enter therapy as they had become increasingly argumentative. Mrs. K. stated that her husband had become less sensitive to her and she gave an example of how she had come to him for support when she was going through a difficult time at work. The job-related problems were so bad that she had experienced feelings of being rejected, frustrated, and helpless. She shared these problems with Mr. K. At first he was very supportive but as time went by and the problem was not only not resolved but daily resurfaced as a topic of painful discourse he became increasingly frustrated. As a last resort he suggested going down to her office and speaking to her supervisors himself—an act which Mrs. K. reasonably refused. He finally gave up and told her that she should take up this issue with someone else. He could not help her.

I was able to help this couple to recognize that in his initial empathetic response to his wife's problem, Mr. K. was feeling her pain. He felt increasingly helpless as the problem continued and he could do nothing to resolve it. When his efforts to solve the problem were ineffective he withdrew. Mr. K. stopped emotionally supporting his wife so that he could stop feeling her pain. I informed the couple that most people are not comfortable with painful and helpless feelings and that it was not unusual for one spouse to take on and try to deal with the problem of the other. However, in appropriating the problem one begins to feel helpless. I suggested that Mr. K. simply provide a safe atmosphere in which Mrs. K. could share her feelings. Mrs. K. would "heal" herself. The psyche will let go of a conflict if there is no distraction from other issues or if no defense mechanisms come into play.

In addition to the problems of not having the training to avoid the natural traps inherent in a new relationship, couples often come into marriage unequipped with adequate communication skills. Partners must learn that they communicate in conscious and unconscious ways and that all behavior is communication. They must learn that unless they are able to clearly communicate their thoughts, feelings and beliefs they will not be able to clarify distortions and misunderstandings nor will they be able to resolve differences.

Further, without effective communication, spouses will be unable to share love, encourage autonomy and experience intimacy. In short, without effective communication skills, couples will have a great deal of difficulty making it past the bargaining stage of marriage.

In summary, the inability to effectively negotiate the initial marital adjustment is, in effect, an inability to allow oneself or one's partner to be free—thereby not allowing for the development of autonomy. A repetitive interactional pattern of not addressing or attacking one another's dignity is established. Phenomenally, the "we psyche" continues to evolve, but in a negative direction, and if not halted, the couple will continue to be caught in a pattern which will lead to emotional distancing and unhappiness.

C. INDIVIDUAL INSECURITIES

Many couples begin their marriage with mutual love and the hope of having a fulfilling relationship, but often the autonomy of one or both partners is not intact. There are many kinds of problems and insecurities which can be brought into marriage. Such problems can include psychotic or personality disorders, the intrusions of parents or former spouses and oppositional behavior from children of former marriages. Psychological insecurities can make spouses defensive, insensitive to the other's needs and rigid and controlling.

Many couples have the unrealistic expectation that marriage should be free from conflict and that success in marriage means continually experiencing romantic feelings toward one another. In a strong marriage, romantic feelings exist, but the relationship is also based on such important dynamics as working through adversity together and providing a secure atmosphere in which both spouses can resolve psychological insecurities. In so doing, partners demonstrate their love for one another while developing mutual trust and respect at the deepest level. The following is a case illustration of this pattern of interaction:

> Mr. and Mrs. A were seen in therapy after they had been married one year. Both were survivors of previous conflictual long term marriages. They felt that the initial feelings that were present at the start of this marriage were deteriorating. In one session Mrs. A stated that the previous evening she had been feeling very insecure and needed more "affection and love" from her husband. He withdrew and she became angry resulting in his becoming defensive. Mr. A maintained that he was not affectionate by nature and Mrs. A was trying to change him into something that he was not. The more she demanded affection from him the more difficulty he experienced in expressing loving feelings. This therapist encouraged Mr. A to explore his wife's insecurities and her need for so much support. During this process, Mrs. A was able to express her feelings of rejection and pain from her first marriage and became very tearful. Mr. A responded spontaneously by reaching out and touching her and then embracing her as she cried. Mrs. A later acknowledged that she had felt supported and loved by Mr. A even though he had not verbally expressed his feelings. She recognized for the first time that love could be shown in non-verbal ways and that her husband was an attentive listener. To reach this point, however, both had to come to the realization that they would have to express insecure feelings rather than demand that the other do something to take away pain. With some help in developing communication skills this couple learned how to draw closer together in a supportive, nurturing relationship.

Couples who are working towards a covenant marital relationship will generally have the capacity to support one another under adverse conditions and to assist each other in resolving problems. However, severe psychological insecurities keep some people self–attentive and prevent them from addressing the needs and feelings of the partner even though they clearly feel love for the other. The more insecure the individual, the greater will be that person's inability to demonstrate the covenant agreements of being a loving witness, being, faithful, speaking the loving truth and making loving gestures. If insecurities are not affectively addressed, there is the likelihood that autonomy and dignity will be diminished. Trust, respect and friendship will eventually be threatened. Finally, the success of the marriage will be put into jeopardy. This is why it is imperative for couples in conflict to seek the early assistance of a marital therapist. Much can be positively accomplished with partners whose love is still intact and whose autonomy and dignity have not been greatly diminished.

> Mr. and Mrs. G. entered therapy ostensibly over a specific issue—that of the wife's desire to have a baby and the husband's resistance to the idea. Mr. G. was severely despondent and had in fact recently quit the teaching profession out of his despair over the institution's ability to teach in what he perceived to be a chaotic world. Mrs. G was unaware of Mr. G's suicidal ideation. Mr. G. described his parents as cruel, uncaring, rigid and alcoholic. When he initially described his childhood he assumed a fetal position and cried hysterically. As he had resisted his wife's attempts to help he was seen alone in therapy.
> Clearly Mr. G needed to deal with his family of origin crises before he could attempt to work on his marriage and he was referred to a psychiatrist for possible antidepressant medication before even this work could begin.

While some therapists do not believe that it is ever important to address family of origin issues, this writer believes that a problem which might have begun thirty years ago remains a problem until it is addressed and resolved. If a client feared his father when he was twelve, it is a current problem if that fear is still causing conflict now that the client is thirty. This therapist believes that all family problems are current issues which may or may not be associated with unresolved past conflicts. This belief allows the writer to accept many of the theoretical concepts developed by Bowen, Boszormenyi-Nagy, Framo, Haley and Minuchin for explicating family development and functioning while utilizing principles of practice supported by Haley and Minuchin for planning and intervention in treatment.

On the surface, the attempt to help clients define an adult relationship with their parents after childhood fears or angers have dominated most of their lives seems like a formidable task. It is possible, if approached correctly, for a client to engage and to be able to resolve family of origin conflicts. I help the client come to the realization that it is possible to take control, establish reasonable expectations and have a realistic relationship with these figures who are real people beyond their role as the client's parent. Often it is a matter of helping the client put in the past the insecurities, feelings of helplessness and constant fight to win the love of the parent. Issues of control are discussed, the feelings of a dependent child and the reality of the adult strength and confidence which can be used to convince the client that it is possible to integrate the past into a new reality in which one can redefine experiences as a mature adult.

Clients often have unrealistic expectations of their parents' ability to love, nurture, or to even behave in a socially acceptable way. It is a fact of love that filial feelings of loyalty transcend even the worst parenting and it is on this loyalty that the therapist can depend when helping clients work on family or origin problems. The therapist must, however, assist the clients in recognizing that they cannot force their parent to make any changes—including developing an ability to show love. But with the knowledge that the parent would have wanted to love them, would have wanted to provide a secure home, would not have consciously hurt them, but did not themselves have all power or wisdom or strength—the client comes to control his/her own relationship with the parent and it becomes possible to integrate negative experiences in a positive way.

Even the worst childhoods had some moments of joy. The client tends to see the past as negative and his/her parents only as "critical parents" with no appreciation for anything good that might have happened. This concept coincides with object–relations theory, which states that children incorporate highlights of reality, either positive or negative, and carry them into their present narrow, often distorted view of what happened. The therapist can help clients broaden their view of reality, correct distortions of the past, and understand parents in their many roles. This can be accomplished by helping clients recognize that many of their positive attributes and strengths come from their early relationship with their parents. It helps the client to learn that there were many factors which were important in their childhood experiences:

1. Parents feel responsibility for growth and development of their children and this becomes manifested in a desire for perfect behavior from the child.

2. Parents invest much of themselves in their children.

3. Child-rearing practices are primarily learned from ones own childhood experiences.

4. Parents have a life apart from child rearing, including having to deal with their own marital relationship.

By encouraging clients to work with their parents, it often becomes evident that the parents also wish to establish a positive relationship. It is an unfortunate reality that many couples have children before they are mature enough to raise a family. Parents of adult children, now mature themselves, often have regrets about some of their behaviors in the past and are anxious to establish a positive adult–to–adult relationship but will rarely initiate the resolution of conflicts because it is difficult to admit ignorance, especially in so important a role.

Therapists can help clients recognize that parents do the best they can and some of the things that happened were unavoidable. Clients often blame their parents for the clients' own weaknesses and behaviors and thus avoid taking responsibility for negative actions and feelings. Blaming also gives them a feeling of control—an explanation for their own inexplicable behavior. This behavior is often later displaced onto the spouse as a device to deal with a dysfunctional marriage.

Mr. G. received anti-depressants after which I helped him to recognize many of the above realities. I encouraged Mr. G. to visit his parents, even though they live in another state. He reluctantly agreed beginning with writing a letter as this was less threatening to him. He was later able to phone them and finally even to visit. In so doing, my client was able to correct past distorted perceptions and to recognize that his role in his family of origin was that of scapegoat. In working with his parents, Mr. G took charge of his feelings, asserted himself, and eventually created autonomy for himself by being able to control his participation in the relationship. His parents actually changed very little, but Mr. G. was able to accept their imperfections. Through this experience Mr. G. was able to transfer his new insights and assertiveness into the marriage relationship. The couple were able to resolve their major differences and decided to have children. It is often the case, however, that when individuals complete family of origin work then they cannot resolve differences in the marriage and will divorce.

In summary, a major building block of the foundation upon which marriage is built is the psychological security of each partner. A happy marriage is comprised of two mature people. One spouse cannot be responsible for maintaining a mutually enhancing relationship. Often marital problems are a result of individual insecurities and these insecurities must be addressed in therapy.

D. FAMILY DEVELOPMENTAL PROBLEMS

Most Americans between the ages of 22 to 26 will have their first child within the first two years of marriage. If they have not moved from the bargaining stage to the enhancement stage of marriage, couples will have difficulty dealing with the family and individual developmental changes which are certain to occur. Rhodes defines the following seven stages in the life cycle of the family:

1. Intimacy vs. idealization or dissolutionment (precedes advent of offspring).
2. Replenishment vs. turning inward (begins with the birth of first child and ends when last child enters school).
3. Individuation of family members vs. pseudomutual organization (families pass through the bearing and rearing of preschool children).

4. Companionship vs. isolation (families with teenage children).

5. Regrouping vs. binding or expulsion (families whose children are leaving home).

6. Rediscovery vs. despair (first of two post-parental phases).

7. Mutual aid vs. uselessness (second post-parental phase.[11]

There are other models of family life cycle, but what they all have in common is the perception that families pass through various stages of growth and that at each stage, roles, functions, tasks, boundaries, caretaking and other factors in the relationship change and will influence the evolution of the marriage. It is useful but not necessary for couples to know the stages of the family life cycle. If a couple is, for example, in an enhancing relationship they will instinctively note changes and adapt and grow accordingly.

Once a child is born, the couple will often fall into the natural trap of losing sight of the marital dyad and will devote up to ninety percent of their time to the parental role. If they have not arrived at the enhancement stage of the marriage, they will lose sight of changes within the family; in the marriage and even in themselves. Adult growth and development does not stop at the age of twenty-one. It is a life process. I believe that adults cannot reach a stable maturity until they have reached at least the age of thirty. Many young adults grow up in their marriage, but are not cognizant of the growth. If couples are not constantly aware of changes in family life cycle and/or individual growth and development, serious problems can arise in the relationship. The following case will illustrate this problem:

> Mr. and Mrs. A. sought marital therapy because of continual arguing. There had been a separation and they were contemplating separating again. Both were college graduates, but Mrs. A chose to be a homemaker after the birth of their first child. Mr. A. loved his wife and she believed in his love, but she was not sure that she was "in love" with him. She knew her husband was a good person but she found herself emotionally estranged from him and the more she attempted to make herself feel loving toward him the less loving she felt. Mr. A. felt his wife's withdrawal and pressured her for more attention, only

succeeding in pushing her further away. After working through her guilt about this situation, Mrs. A. agreed to a structured separation to try to discover what her real feelings were.

The couple were in the integration phase of marriage when their problems began. Both agreed that they had a happy and satisfying relationship during the first eight years of their marriage. Mrs. A. enjoyed her homemaking tasks and her husband his business responsibilities. The couple spent little time together as Mr. A. had to work long hours to keep up with his position as corporate president. The couple took an annual vacation at which time they had time to renew their loving relationship.

A major change occurred in the family routine during the third or "individuation of family members vs. pseudomutual organization" phase of family development. At the time the couple's second and last child entered grammar school, creating feelings of restlessness within Mrs. A. In an effort to do something about the problem, Mr. and Mrs. A. started a business together. The problems grew worse. The following excerpt from a session illustrates Mrs. A's growing understanding of the development of the problem.

> After being home with the kids for so long I felt so stagnated. Everything I said was in two syllable words and I felt so inadequate being around other people other than my immediate family. T. and I would go out with business associates and I always felt I didn't really communicate . . . T. and I would discuss kids or nothing and I was really getting a low opinion of myself. There was something I wanted to prove. I realized that I needed to use my brain for other things. T. taught me a lot . . . I really learned a lot . . . but once I learned it it was really boring to me. The bonus—at the time I thought it was a bonus, was that I started feeling attractive to other men and, um . . . it was nice. It was nice because as I said at the time I had a low opinion of myself . . . but T. still didn't notice me. I started changing—having my nails done and spending a lot of money on clothes. T. never noticed a new hairstyle or if I had my nails done. But I was getting positive feedback from other people and I liked that. I would rather have had it from my husband. But it did help raise my opinion of myself.

In therapy, Mrs. A. recognized that during the course of her marriage she had developed into a "mature woman." She believed, however, that her responsibilities of homemaker did not reflect her maturity or competency and this resulted in feelings of inadequacy and poor self-esteem. She experienced success with her business which helped her to feel competent, mature and autonomous. But the romantic attention she received from men made her husband jealous. Consequently, instead of encouraging her, he became possessive and controlling. This led to continued arguing and strengthened Mrs. A's doubt about her love for her husband. Her belief that she must stay in the marriage at any cost only created more frustration and distancing.

The separation allowed Mrs. A. to feel autonomous and to recognize that she was not "trapped" in the marriage. With her new insight, positive feelings about herself and the support and encouragement of her husband who had resolved his insecurities, Mrs. A. found herself "falling in love" with Mr. A.

In summary, Mr. and Mrs. A. as is the case with married couples, remained in the integration phase of the marital development and consequently were vulnerable to individual and family developmental crises. Mrs. A. began to feel insecure because she felt stagnated in her development as a person. The insecurity manifested itself when her youngest child entered school, leaving her with time on her hands. She started a business with her husband in order to achieve self-enhancement. This raised her level of confidence, creating marital and emotional distancing, to the point where divorce was contemplated. With the assistance of marital therapy, Mrs. A. was able to resolve her ambivalence about the marriage.

Couples who reach the integration phase of marital development often do not recognize that their marriage can be much more satisfying than it is. As a result, they begin to drift emotionally apart by ignoring the husband/wife relationship. The foundation upon which the relationship has been built has been weakened. The vulnerability of the marriage is not exposed until they are faced with a situational change or a crisis. They must continue to build on their relationship as husband and wife if autonomy is to be maintained, dignity reinforced and the "we psyche" moved in a positive direction.

E. SITUATIONAL PROBLEMS

Couples who have not developed beyond the integration phase of marital development are vulnerable to situational changes such as job loss, physical disability, relocation or death in the family. Situational changes can create major disruption in family interaction. Spouses will escalate their expectations of emotional support. During a crisis couples often find that they have drifted apart and they cannot reclaim former feelings when the crisis has passed. In the case of shared expectations, sometimes the realization of the dream is a change that cannot sustain the hope. When, for example, one spouse is going to college and the other is supporting the family, they are working harmoniously toward a common goal. But after the spouse who was a student graduates and they at least have time to plan a future together, they often feel that they do not know each other. The student has lived at the library and the spouse has built an independent life. The only thing they had in common was the striving toward the goal.

> Mr. and Mrs. M had another situational problem: They entered therapy because of a pattern of constant conflict. Both were college graduates, but Mrs. M. had elected to be a homemaker until her youngest child was in Jr. High. This was a stipulation of the marriage mandated by Mr. M. who felt very strongly that a mother should be home with her children. Mrs. M's mother, with whom she had been very close, had died the previous year. Shortly after her mother's death Mrs. M. decided that she felt compelled to return to her career as a teacher. She did so against her husband's express wishes. He felt betrayed by her action and constantly pressured her to quit work. She felt negated and attacked and believed her husband to be unreasonable. They had not resolved these differences in three months and the anger was beginning to affect other issues of their relationship.

Mr. and Mrs. M. had had a peaceful, loving relationship until this first major crisis. They were not, however in an enhancing phase of marriage and seldom did things together. The death of Mrs. M's mother exposed the vulnerability of the marriage. The couple was not in the habit of sharing feelings, and insecurities and they had no problem solving skills to resolve the issue of Mrs. M's return to work. Through various interventions, the couple was able to learn to recognize and thus empathize with each other's pain and insecurities. They are learning to successfully resolve their differences.

In summary, couples who have drifted apart in the integration phase of marriage are not attentive to each other's needs and desires. They lose sight of the state of being loving witnesses to each other, speaking in loving truth and making loving gestures. They stop being loving friends. Consequently, the foundation of the marriage is weakened and the relationship becomes vulnerable to situational crisis or change. Fortunately, Mr. and Mrs. M were able to reclaim the loving relationship that they had once enjoyed.

8

THE
NEGATIVE SPIRAL

IN STRUCTURE, THE "NEGATIVE SPIRAL" is like the chambered Nautilus shell, with its benign wide opening an easy attraction, but turn by turns, its coils becoming tighter until it ends in a dark tight place with no light, and so convoluted that escape seems impossible. In sensation, once deep within the negative spiral, the couple feels caught in a whirlpool:

> The mating of rising and falling oceanic tides . . . in its frenzied downward spiral the eddy will pull in all objects, as if to nourish itself. The whirlpool, seemingly independent of the sea, enters a confused and destructive state, indiscriminately swallowing and digesting debris. It is, perhaps, a spiral gone awry, swept away by its own motion.[12]

No matter how marital problems begin, a negative spiral syndrome develops and the more dysfunctional the relationship, the deeper enmeshed in the spiral the couple will become. At the first coil of the spiral is disagreement. If this is not resolved it will lead to anger—the next turn is criticism—leading to a wish to control—which turns into defensiveness—twisting into insecurity—deepening into lack of trust—leading to resentment—and ending in the abyss—the death of love.

The sequencing of the feelings and behaviors might not follow in this order and could be concurrent. Nevertheless, if this dysfunctional pattern of interacting does not reverse itself the couple will be pulled further into the negative spiral.

Diagram II
Characteristics of the Negative Spiral Syndrome

	Shallow	Moderately Deep	Deep	Abyss
1. Conflict				
A. Frequency	few x a week	several x week	almost daily	daily
B. Issue vs. Person	mostly issue	both issue and person	mostly person	person
C. Specificity	one issue	many issues	most issues	everything
D. Location	in private	with family	with friends	in public
E. Resolution	immediate	before morning	seldom	never
2. Anger				
A. Intensity	mild	moderate	strong	intense
B. Frustration Level	mild	moderate	strong	intense
3. Criticism				
A. Intensity	mild	moderate	strong	intense
B. Frequency	few x week	several x week	almost daily	daily
C. Specificity	one issue	many issues	most issues	everything
D. Issues vs. Person	issue focused	issues & person	mostly person	person
E. Location	in private	with family	with friends	in public
4. Control				
A. Areas	behavior	beliefs	feelings	thoughts
5. Defensiveness				
A. Communication	fair	poor	very poor	extremely poor
6. Insecurity				
A. Degree of feeling safe with self	mild	moderate	minimal	unsafe
B. Degree of feeling safe with spouse	mild	moderate	minimal	unsafe
7. Trust				
A. Emotional needs	occasionally	seldom	rarely	never
B. Physical needs	occasionally	seldom	rarely	never
8. Resentment				
A. Level	mild	moderate	strong	intense

Anger

In dysfunctional relationships there is an underlying feeling of anger which is continuously felt. Partners who feel ignored or attacked are unable to resolve differences. They anticipate being rejected or criticized by the spouse. The intensity of the anger and the frustration tolerance of the partners influence this interaction. If the angry feelings are not intense and where frustration tolerance is high, there will be little expressed criticism. On the other hand, if there are very strong feelings of anger and frustration tolerance is low, criticism will be strongly manifested. But not all people express anger in criticism. The anger might be manifested by withdrawal of affection or by passive-aggressive actions. In evaluating the couple, one must always be aware of the couple's particular way of expressing anger.

Criticism

No one welcomes unwarranted or inappropriate criticism. Such an attack naturally creates anger and defensiveness. An attack on a spouse is an attack on that partner's autonomy and dignity. Implied, even if not explicitly stated, is that the person is stupid, dishonest or insensitive. The partner is motivated to counterattack and argumentative behavior is escalated. The variables associated with criticism include the intensity of the criticism, its frequency, and whether it is general or specifically directed. Whether the criticism is issue–centered or directed at the character of the partner must be taken into consideration when evaluating dysfunctional interactional patterns. In enhancing marriages, there is little criticism. Instead, partners share and examine common issues out of a desire to be attentive and respectful toward one another. Because no ill feelings are nurtured, issues are resolved quickly and effectively. Criticism is gentle and usually issue oriented. Problem resolution takes place privately.

In dysfunctional relationships, issues are not resolved. Partners harbor angry feelings and experience continual frustration and help-lessness. As a result, criticism is intense and frequent. The criticism is directed toward issues and also the partner's character. It erupts constantly, sometimes even in public places.

Cultural factors must be considered in assessing the expression of criticism in a relationship. In some cultures, criticism is expected and is interpreted as a display of love and concern. Even within these cultures, however, the criticism is not normally a direct demeaning attack of the partner's dignity.

Control

In order to successfully negotiate the many differences partners bring into a relationship and to adapt to the changes and crises that will inevitably occur, flexibility is imperative. In being amenable to change, partners encourage their spouses to freely express thoughts and feelings. In so doing, the dignity of each partner will be maintained and autonomy facilitated. Conversely, when partners are dogmatic and rigid, individual freedom is stifled and an interactional pattern which is based on control will develop. The more control attempted in a marriage, the less care and concern for the partner is manifested. The dignity of the partner is attacked and autonomy threatened.

The underlying dynamic of control is either characterological or developmental and comes out of helplessness or fear. These feelings are generally associated with the belief that one is unable to influence one's partner, that the partner is not concerned about meeting the spouse's needs, but rather must be coerced into any positive action. Such a belief can be conscious or unconscious and based in reality, fantasy, or both. It can be rooted in family of origin issues, psychological insecurities, or distrust which has developed within the marriage. In any case, most people will respond to control either by attempting to counter control, by resistance, or passive aggressive behavior. In cases where one spouse is able to control the other, there is little satisfaction gained from the control. Angry feelings and resentment are repressed by the passive partner which results in emotional distancing and deeper feelings of mistrust. The underlying belief and fear in the controlling spouse remains the same, as that person can only become secure when freely attended. In most cases, the control that is exhibited reflects the intensity of the belief that the controlled spouse is incapable of meeting needs out of feelings of love.

Attempts at control are manifested in many ways. Some partners will withhold information, lie, or threaten. Others will attempt bribery, manipulate and exhibit passive–aggressive behavior. Some will resort to verbal and sometimes physical abuse. Although most people recognize at some level that this kind of controlling behavior is an affront to their dignity, some controlling partners admit they do not like behaving in this way and the blame is inevitably shifted to the partner.

In relationships not caught in the negative spiral, there is very little effort to control. In marriages which are caught in the spiral, control is first displayed as an attempt to control behavior. Heading toward the abyss, there is more and more effort at controlling everything about the partner. Partners are told with whom they can develop a relationship, what they must wear, where they are allowed to go and how much they can spend. I had one client who instructed his wife about what kind of nylons she could buy. As the marriage deteriorates, partners will attempt to control their spouse's beliefs, feelings, and even thoughts.

Defensiveness

It is normal to become defensive when one is experiencing conflict, threatened with angry expressions of feelings, being criticized and not given freedom. Defensive partners cannot respond in a reasonable or supportive way. Psychological defense mechanisms such as projection, repression, denial or displacement are manifested. Partners begin to use dysfunctional coping mechanisms such as blaming, counterattacking or becoming workaholic to cope with their emotional pain. As a result, the ability to communicate in a mature way declines. The greater the defensiveness, the less the ability to hear, understand, validate or support the partner. There is no possibility of real communication.

Couples become argumentative when communication is poor, but eventually they are able to hear and understand one another and differences can be resolved. When communication is very poor, couples can still hear and understand one another, but they begin to lose the ability to validate or support the other's view or to successfully problem solve. Dysfunctional coping mechanisms begin to have greater influence in the interactional pattern. Couples displaying minimal communication do not accept that what their partner is saying has any validity at all. There is minimal ability to negotiate differences. When couples manifest profoundly poor communication, interactions become argumentative.

Interpretations of events, actions and behaviors are viewed differently. Partners discount or correct everything that is said. There is a lack of conflict resolution and even benign gestures are seen as negative or manipulative.

Insecurity

As the foundation of the relationship deteriorates, the partners' feelings of being secure about themselves and feeling safe in the relationship begin to erode. Spouses begin to doubt their observational abilities, their own and their partner's personality traits and needs. One wife in such a relationship reported that she was unable to make accurate judgements, was beginning to doubt who she was and what was normal to expect from a marriage. This woman is a competent professional, has many caring friends and is respected throughout the community.

It is normal for spouses to feel insecure about themselves when they are continually confronted with or are displaying criticism, conflict and dysfunctional coping mechanisms in their marriage. A "loving witness" will enhance the dignity and autonomy of his or her partner. Conversely, living with or being a "critical witness" begins a process which impoverishes the dignity and autonomy of each partner. In extremely dysfunctional marriages it is likely that both partners have constant feelings of insecurity.

As the relationship becomes more conflictual, spouses will begin to feel less safe with their partner. They will become afraid of sharing their inner self, believing that they will not be supported and validated. As the marriage continues to descend into the "negative spiral" the couple will lose the hope of being attended to by the partner. This will often lead them to seek support and comfort from family, friends or colleagues. In extreme cases, spouses will become involved in an affair to find the nurturance and validation which is lacking in the marriage.

Trust

Trust is necessary for the development of an enhancing relationship. Without trust, a partner cannot be secure in the feeling of being loved. Without trust, there can be no security in the expectation that the partner will be attentive, will be faithful and will offer loving gifts. In enhancing marriages, loving gestures are given daily, and profound trust is in place. In conflictual relationships, angry feelings are part of the normal pattern, freedom is stifled and trust is quickly lost.

Meeting emotional needs includes the will to support a partner's aspirations, ambitions and dreams. It also requires that the partner be available in a time of crisis. It is the absolute knowledge that the partner is your best friend and will always act in your interest. Meeting physical needs includes sharing the responsibilities of a household, earning a living, sharing in the caretaking and nurturance of children and enjoying a full and mutually fulfilling sexual life.

In marriages where there is a moderate amount of trust, spouses will at times suspect their partner's motives or intentions. The reliability of one's partner may come to be questioned, but there is an overall belief in the trustworthiness of the other. Where there is little trust between partners, there is constant questioning about the reliability and intentions of the partner. The lack of trust will lead to attempts to control behavior. When there is minimal trust, spouses will either stop relying on their partner or they will become highly critical. In such relationships, partners do not believe anything that is told them, do not trust their partner's intentions, and become involved in "mind reading" the thoughts and feelings of the other. There is no ability to problem solve because there is no credibility. Some partners live in the constant fear that any remark they might make will be attacked.

Resentment

Resentment contributes more than any other feeling to the descent into the abyss. Resentment is generally the end result of cumulative anger, bitterness, mistrust, and disappointment. Through the years these feelings propel the couple into the spiral—the years of arguments, lack of attentiveness, and attacks on dignity and autonomy. In a recent case, I asked the spouses to list the things that they resented in their ten years of marriage. The wife listed thirty–two complaints and indicated to her husband that she could not forgive him for most of the things listed. The couple proceeded in divorce therapy.

Resentment perpetuates the expression of anger and criticism, fosters defensiveness and destroys trust. When resentment is mild, the underlying feelings are anger, frustration, and helplessness. As the resentment goes deeper, they turn into feelings of being offended and betrayed. When there is deep resentment, spouses will feel outraged and victimized. Finally, when profound resentment is evident, the partners will feel the chaotic whirlpool of despair.

SUMMARY

In summary, couples caught in the "negative spiral" will feel increasingly helpless and frustrated at every turn. The internalization of the anger usually takes the form of attacking and blaming the partner. Inherent is the message, "You change," which is felt by the receiver of the message as an attempt to control. The spouse will counterattack somehow but the message becomes internalized. Feelings of safety diminish which leads to a lack of trust. What is stated is not accepted as true. Mind–reading develops. A pattern of trying to "win" arguments will develop. Unresolved arguments will lead to resentment—a feeling that is destructive to love. This loss of loving feelings perpetuates conflict and the spiral tightens. The result is the abyss of emotional divorce.

III

The Model of
Constructual Marital Therapy

9

INTRODUCTION
TO
THE MODEL

CONSTRUCTUAL MARITAL THERAPY was developed in the recognition that most marital therapists are eclectic in their practice. They do not rely on just one theory to define marital growth and behavior or to establish principles of practice. There are many variables which determine human behavior including, but not limited to physical appearance, self-perception, learned behaviors, and capacity for learning.

Couples also have unique characteristics, such as patterns of communication, organizational structure, depth of loyalty and coping mechanisms. Dysfunctional families tend to develop an infinite variety of painful interactions and behaviors. A covenant relationship is constant and easily recognizable as such. In the words of Leo Tolstoy:

> All happy families are alike—every unhappy family is unhappy in
> its own way.[13]

Couples respond to environmental influences such as social, cultural, political, educational and economic superstructures. The infinite interactions between self, spouse and environment assure that every marriage will be constantly influenced by change. The couple is not only influenced by present circumstances, but past influences often have considerable relevance to the present marital dynamic.

Given the abundance of variables which influence behavior, it is clear that no one model, unless it allows for eclectic interventions, can attempt to meet the needs of all marital problems.

Integrating models of therapy can be very complex and difficult.[14] However CMT offers the advantage of allowing therapists the freedom to select a concept from one theoretician, principle of practice from another and techniques from a third in order to meet the unique needs of their clients. Instead of being instructed to conform to a given treatment orientation regardless of problem, ethnicity, family constellation or socio–economic condition, clients will benefit by being able to utilize many treatment plans within a pliable framework.

Because CMT helps therapists to better understand the various subsystems operative in families, it can also assist in establishing guiding principles of practice. This will make it easier to focus on appropriate subsystems as necessary. These principles will help the therapist work more freely with:

1. the marriage relative to external factors
2. the nuclear family
3. the extended family
4. various family subgroups
5. the individual relative to the marriage
6. the family of origin

CMT will provide a framework which will help the therapist to determine the appropriate subsystem on which to focus for the best therapeutic result.

Further, CMT encourages therapists to be multi–dimensional, taking into consideration cognitive, affective, behavioral, systems dynamics and therapeutic approaches. Many therapists have knowledge of a variety of techniques but fail to maximize their options. Multi–dimensional approaches, on the other hand, allow for a shifting of emphasis from one approach to another as is appropriate situationally. This inter–connection of approaches can occur in one session or over a period of time.

Finally, CMT encourages therapists' sensitivity toward the multitude of thoughts and feelings inherent in each client and each situation, and a recognition that there is simultaneous communication occurring at many levels.

A constant awareness of these processes increases the therapists confidence in his/her ability to accomplish several tasks concurrently. Often, a single therapeutic intervention will facilitate a domino effect of positive change in many inter–related problem areas.

It requires a very broad base of knowledge to become a Constructual Family Therapist. Knowledge of specific principles and techniques will be enhanced by participation in seminars, workshops, classes, and the reading of professional literature.

CMT divides the information base necessary to diagnoses and treatment of couples in conflict into five categories:

1. values
2. facts
3. holistic therapeutic models
4. specialized therapeutic models
5. theories

A. VALUES

No matter how objective a therapist might try to be, each will bring his/her own values into their therapeutic practice. Even our selection of theories is born of our value system as theories are, by definition, not facts. We must make decisions based on subjective reality. Therapists will often project their values onto the couple. A therapist with a high regard for the value of responsibility might say or imply to a couple "It is your responsibility to stay with your wife because she is trying to make the marriage work." It is inappropriate for therapists to impose their own values on clients. Further, couples often feel vulnerable and helpless and will grasp at any firm directive as received truth. Irreparable harm is possible in such cases.

There are three ways in which we can minimize the misuse of our own personal value system when we are working with couples. First, I cannot over emphasis the importance of good training. A beginning therapist must, under supervision, be exposed to actual cases in progress. Videotapes provide excellent training if viewed with a skilled supervisor. Secondly, therapists need to have a strong theoretical base. Without such a base, the therapist will find data confusing, uninteresting and unhelpful. Without a firm grounding in theory, one can only view phenomena from personal experience, making us as effective as relatives, bartenders and hairdressers. (Which is not to say that these lay people do not have an enviable record of success). I am of the belief that the more we draw from personal experience in our interventions, the more we are subject to imposing our value system on the couple.

Finally, the therapist must constantly monitor his/her approach to determine if strongly held personal ethical standards for behavior have been allowed to overly influence practice principles in couples interventions.

It is inevitable that we will rely to some degree on our personal ethical values. The initial interview is the best time to explain our understanding of a mature relationship, what is required to achieve this goal and our treatment plan. The implicit value system within the definition of the relationship will be clear to the couple. They are then able to make an informed decision to remain with us or seek help elsewhere.

B. FACTS

Therapists must pay attention to the factual information which is revealed in therapy and the affect this information will have on the marital relationship. Too often therapists extrapolate simple statements of fact into theoretical formulations. A common manifestation of this is when a spouse refuses to leave an extremely dysfunctional relationship in the full knowledge that it will never change. Many therapists will interpret this as representative of psychological insecurity rather than a true dilemma and will dredge up theoretical formulations to substantiate the diagnosis. Couples are often faced with choices which have major unpleasant consequences no matter what action is taken. It is hard for some therapists to come to the realization that they cannot solve all problems brought into their office.

Therapists are also capable of forgetting that theories are to be used as devices to help them understand human dynamics and instead they treat theoretical concepts as if they were received wisdom. In so doing, their approach to marital therapy becomes rigid. Finally, some therapists are simply unable to recognize their client's limitations. I have observed therapists pushing clients to recognize "deeper feelings" when the client was incapable of communicating in this way.

I remember one interview where a therapist was urging a client to "get in touch with his feelings." The client responded, "Look, Dr. M., I know that you are trying to get me to see something in myself, but you are going to have to give me multiple choices!" The client was more aware of his limitations than was the therapist.

C. HOLISTIC THERAPEUTIC MODELS

Holistic therapeutic models are those models of practice which can be applied to any couple and where theoretical concepts, principles of practice, and techniques are integrated. Such models include: Bowen Family Therapy, Structural Family Therapy, Contextual Family Therapy, Sagers' Contracting and Strategic Therapy. Constructual Family therapists are free to select from these models and others, as theoretical concepts, principles of practice and techniques are treated as independent variables. One can, for example, create differentiation (a Bowen concept) by using structural or strategic interventions.

D. SPECIALIZED THERAPEUTIC MODELS

Specialized therapeutic models are those models of practice which are applicable to special situations and problems. Models of this practice, for example, deal with alcoholism, grief, domestic violence, and sex abuse.

E. THEORIES

The general public is of the unfortunate opinion that therapy is simply the giving of informed advice. One of my relatives once commented "Why are they paying you all that money when I can give the same advice for nothing?" Often, couples have sought the advice of their pediatrician, hairdresser or bartender who usually has given "good common sense advice" which they do not follow. Professional help is sought when these avenues are exhausted. The therapist has specialized training which allows for an understanding of the underlying dynamics of theoretical formulations associated with bonding, intimacy, intrapsychic dynamics, anger, violence, etc.

F. SUMMARY

In summary, as illustrated in Diagram III, therapists must have access to a vast amount of knowledge. This knowledge can be stored on metaphorical tapes in the mind or actual tapes or books in a library— but it must be accessible information. When a client comes in with problem "A," a good therapist will be able to pull a tape called "Information, Research and Practice Principles Proven Effective in Cases of Problem 'A.'"

Diagram III
Examples of Theoretical Tapes

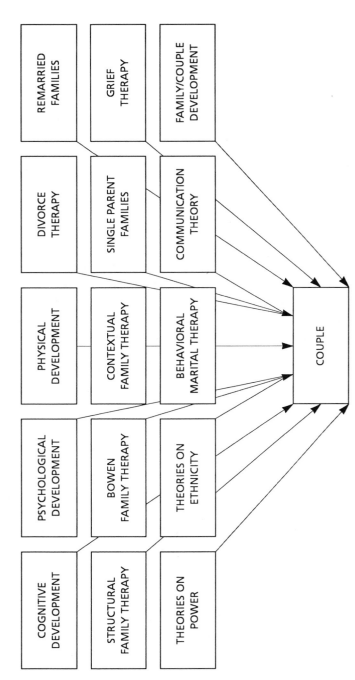

10

PROCESS OF CONSTRUCTUAL MARITAL THERAPY

CMT IS A COMPLEX PROCESS involving therapists, the couples they treat, and sometimes the couples' friends, children, or extended families, as well as other professionals or institutions. It is, therefore, important for therapists to be flexible and open to using various modes for intervening. It is also important for them to be clear regarding the objectives of marital therapy, their roles as therapists, the course of therapy, and marital therapy principle of practice.

A. OBJECTIVES OF MARITAL THERAPY

Therapy is, by definition, treatment. Couples resort to marital treatment only after the symptoms have become very painful. Often couples come into therapy with the expectation that they will be given a psychological analgesic to take away all their pain or even that the therapist will administer a magical cure. But what therapy does, all it can do, is provide a safe and neutral clinical atmosphere in which couples can be directed to define, examine and discuss issues and expectations and communicate personal truth. Sometimes the "cure" is major surgery as the couple discovers that they do not love each other and that divorce is the only way that they can go on to lead healthy lives.

Some couples confuse therapy with the giving of specific instructions and they expect to be handed a prescription for finding happiness. There is no known cure for an unhappy marriage. In the absence of a specific cure, there are a thousand nostrums offered. They proliferate our bookstores and talk shows and even surface in some kinds of therapy.

What effective therapy can do is to help to empower a couple to use their own abilities and insights to help themselves. They know each other in ways no therapist could. They know what "buttons to push" to get a negative response. They need to apply that kind of knowledge and power to positive interactions.

In brief, marital therapy is an interactional process between a couple and a therapist with the objective of resolving the couple's differences. During that process, the hope is that distortions are corrected, fears are overcome, objective truth is discovered and trust is established. In truly successful interventions positive methods of problem resolution are discovered and the maximum fulfillment possible for the relationship is achieved.

B. ROLE OF THE THERAPIST

The role of the marital therapist is to use his/her body of knowledge and clinical skills to facilitate a process of interaction between spouses which will direct them toward solving whatever problems they bring into therapy. We know that the reason they are there is they have been unable to solve their problems themselves and their relationship is leading down the spiral staircase. It is the responsibility of therapists to assist clients to:

1. See new insights in themselves and their relationship
2. Develop new skills for the resolution of issues and conflicts
3. Develop a mature pattern of relating to each other.

We believe that the therapist must always be aware of the dignity and goodness inherent in each person and we must assume that every client wishes, at some level, to behave in a respectful, warm and mature manner and wishes to be the recipient of such behavior from his/her partner. It might not appear this way as we observe couples screaming obscenities at each other or accusing each other of purposefully malicious behaviors. In extreme cases, couples are so verbally abusive they get thrown out of restaurants or so physically abusive they end up in emergency rooms. We must not lose sight of the frustration, helplessness and insecurity which are the operative defense mechanisms at work in these dysfunctional behaviors.

All spouses want a positive relationship, even those who appear to define themselves by their level of misery. The are not "happy to be unhappy" but are so insecure, either in themselves or the relationship that they become stuck in their negative feelings and behaviors. They are wallowing in the mud of the relationship because they have lost sight of the dry land and they feel that to let go would be to drown. And they remain stuck because in some cases they do not realize that, with a little more strength, they could pull themselves out of the mud and find a much more pleasant place to be. Even if that means leaving the relationship.

Therapists must always strive to be objective. We know this, but it is hard to achieve because of counter–transference, and personal standards of acceptable behavior. All of us have thought at least once "How awful it would be to be married to that person." However it is the responsibility of therapists to make judgements and to use those judgements to assist clients in finding their truth, overcome fears, recognize themselves and their defense mechanisms and to create understanding between spouses.

We may believe there is no love in the marriage or even that the relationship is potentially harmful, but we must respect the spouse's right to self–determination. If we are skilled, we can sometimes help them to find healthy solutions to their problems. But we are not judges and we cannot demand change.

We can treat clients in a respectful supportive and caring way even if we disagree with their personal ethics, attitudes or behaviors. But if we do not experience genuine concern for their welfare we must remove ourselves from the case. If we continue to see them, even in a genuine effort to help, our bias will render us ineffective.

C. THE COURSE OF THERAPY

By the very act of working with a particular couple the therapist will become a part of that marital system. There are rare cases in which a therapist is given absolute power by the couple. They are so helpless that they are vulnerable to the slightest suggestion. However, in most cases, therapists have little power to create change but can influence behavior if they are trusted and respected by the client. We know that we are no different from the people who come to us. We have often demonstrated the very behaviors we see before us. The only difference is we have some knowledge and expertise in the area of human interaction. We must never lose sight of the fact the people we see are trusting us with their pain, their secrets, their vulnerabilities and sometimes their most important life decisions.

A major goal of any kind of therapy is to minimize resistance. The best way to do this is to treat clients with care, respect and support. Additionally, CMT emphasizes the positive aspects of the interactions as this tact is more conducive to change. CMT is not blind to negative behavior, it simply looks in another direction. If we focus on the strengths, not the weaknesses of a relationship the couple will often realize that they were not seeing their relationship clearly.

We must help clients to see their own goodness, strengths and abilities. If we can accomplish this we will provide a more fertile field for the deep–seeding of respect and trust. It will also help to empower the couple which will minimize their tendency to create an unhealthy dependency on us.

CMT encourages couples to relate to one another in an interactional manner. Emphasis is on process rather than content. Ideally, couples will learn to communicate with one another about their feelings, beliefs, dreams and pain. We might have to take on several roles to accomplish this goal, including the roles of broker, educator, interpreter, advocate or explorer. But our starting role is the one of facilitator.

D. PRINCIPLES OF PRACTICE

Constructual Marital Therapists have a primary set of practice principles from which to draw in clinical interventions. These principles are derived from other therapeutic models, particularly structural and strategic family interventions, and from the writer's clinical experience. These principles reflect what I believe to be the objective of marital therapy, the role of the therapist, and how therapy should be conducted.

The following principles of practice are general guidelines for therapists dealing with couples in conflict. They are not fixed rules. The more experienced you become, the more you will deviate from the rules.

Table I
Constructual Principles of Practice

1. Create a positive atmosphere:
The key for facilitating growth in a relationship is for the therapist to create an emotional environment in which clients feel comfortable and open to change.

2. Join with the clients:
Joining is an active effort on the part of the therapist to show clients they are cared about as individuals and that the therapist supports, understands, empathizes with and is in many ways like them.

3. Begin with presenting problem:
Clients come in with an agenda and specific expectations from therapy. Accept whatever the client offers. This is what you are being trusted with at the moment. Motivation for moving ahead increases as the couple gains control over the presenting problem. (The one exception to this practice principle is when the presenting problem is clearly non–negotiable).

4. Accept role as expert:
Clients attend therapy expecting the clinician to be an expert in marital therapy. The clinician needs to accept that responsibility. In so doing, the therapist maintains control in sessions and couples are confident that they will be helped.

5. Avoid non-negotiable issues:
A couple often has an on going conflict on which they hold non–negotiable positions. To address such issues will only continue conflict. Instead, begin with less emotionally charged issues which the couple can successfully problem solve.

---

6. Be cautious in using feeling statements:
Many clients feel threatened and uncomfortable when asked to identify feelings. Address the clients at the level of your perception of their emotional literacy.

7. Avoid accepting a one–sided viewpoint:
The therapist must always compare the different views the partners' have of the problem. This helps identify differences in awareness of the relationship, allows for acceptance of personal perception and minimizes the clients fear that the therapist is siding with the other partner.

8. Involve and then dismiss significant others:
It is a good practice to bring in family/friends early in therapy to establish areas of conflict and support. It is easier to dismiss support people from therapy than it is to bring them in once the work has begun.

9 Do not rescue:
There are times when one partner is experiencing intense emotional pain and the partner does not respond appropriately or we might believe that one partner is being treated unfairly by the other. In being part of such interactions the impulse of the therapist is to "rescue" the person in pain. However, in so doing the therapist would be siding and thereby negating effective problem solving by the couple.

10. Be in control but not center stage:
For effective utilization of time, the session should focus on facilitating communication between the partners. When the therapist intervenes, it should be for the purpose of directing interactions through interventions which initiate clearer communication of the partners' thoughts and feelings.

11. Work on one problem at a time:
In order to keep the clients focused in the therapeutic process, it is necessary to work on one problem at a time. This prevents the therapist from offering a "shotgun" approach to the problems in the relationship and helps both client and therapist avoid being overwhelmed by a myriad of complex issues.

12. Schedule change–oriented interventions:
Well–planned sessions encourage the therapist to be organized and focused which helps to quickly achieve positive change, thus re–enforcing the clients confidence in the therapeutic process.

13. Identify and build on strengths:
There are positive aspects to even the most dysfunctional relationship. Individual and couples' strengths are important guidelines for effective

action. Focusing on strengths helps to develop individual self–esteem
and initiates healthy change. Some couples are so invested in negative
interactions that they have forgotten the positive aspects of their
relationship.

14. Translate feelings into actions:
Clients generally identify problems in non-descriptive terms or as
"feelings" which often leads to an inability to take corrective measures.
To modify such situations, the therapist should involve the couple in
identifying problems in behavioral terms and then move toward a
course of "actions" which will lead to change.

15. Quickly involve both spouses in treatment:
The longer a therapist works with only one spouse, the more the other
spouse will identify the therapist with the partner.

16. Build Bridges:
Couples participating in marital therapy might be so distanced that they
believe there is no reason for staying together. By "building bridges"
the therapist attempts to reduce the emotional distancing by showing
the couples ways in which they do care for each other and share beliefs
and feeling which can be the building blocks for a happier, more
successful marriage.

17. Direct relationships toward symmetry:
Couples sometimes develop an inverse relationship characterized by
inequality stemming from a one up or one down position in which the
therapist has the couple move toward a mutual exchange of inter-acting
patterns characterized by equality.

18. Be aware of your messages:
The therapist should be aware of his/her body posture, educational level
of speaking, tone of voice and non–verbal communications. A therapist
can move his/her seat to show support or distance and join with the
client by imitating non–verbal cues, i.e., take off coat, put hand under
chin, fold hands.

19. Control the session:
The therapist takes charge of the dialogue in the session by allowing
content which provides different levels of feelings, intensity or volume
of verbal communication. The therapist also maintains a balance of time
so that one client does not dominate.

20. Move from content to process:
Constructual Therapy emphasizes a process rather than a
"understanding" approach to marital counselling. The working
assumption of many therapists is that insight leads to change. This may
or may not be true. The more dysfunctional a couple is the less helpful is

the "understanding" approach. Constructual therapy proposes that for many clients, involvement in a process which leads them to interact in a different way is a more positive intervention than is education alone.

21. Do not get locked into content:

Often a problem presented by the couple is fascinating and might even be similar to a problem faced by the therapist. We must remember that we cannot focus on the issue alone but must instead help the couple address the dynamics of behavior and attitude which will lead them to problem solve on their own.

11

CHOOSING
A METHOD

HISTORICALLY, THE MARITAL THERAPY METHOD of choice was the concurrent method. (The therapist sees each partner separately). This was due to the early influence of psychoanalytic theory. In the 1960's therapists began seeing spouses conjointly (together). the seventies brought an assortment of methods including: combined therapy (a combination of concurrent and conjoint), collaborative (partners are seen by different therapists) and combined/collaborative (the individual therapists occasionally meet together with the partners). There is no clear evidence of the impact of these methods on the outcome of the marriage, but one study did indicate the following:

> Conjoint therapy was most successful for those couples who remained married but produced the poorest outcome for those who obtained divorces. . . . Individual interview were the worst for those remaining married, but ranked second best for those who obtained divorces. Concurrent therapy, which was the most common marital therapy at the time, was worst overall, ranking last for those who remained married and second to last for those who turned to divorce.[15]

Although we do not know the precise impact these different therapies have on the outcome of treatment, we recognize that these methods do influence the relationship and interactional patterns between spouses and among spouses and their therapist(s). They also influence the direction of the therapy and thus its outcome. It is therefore, essential for therapists to be aware of these influences when choosing a method.

A. CONJOINT THERAPY

There are three factors which make it difficult to work with couples conjointly. First, most couples come into therapy with intense feelings of anger, frustration, resentment and hurt. In session, these feelings become translated into blaming, accusing, rigid positioning, denial of responsibility, and sometimes verbal abuse. It may appear that these couples are interested only in winning arguments and have no wish to hear, understand or validate each other. A skilled therapist can use this energy and intensity to initiate effective therapeutic interventions.

Secondly, any therapist finds it difficult "tracking" information between argumentative couples who are in the process of changing the subject, acting out defensively and are in a circular pattern of attacking and counter-attacking. Therapists must somehow grab onto substantive issues from the barrage of information flying around the room and focus the couple on these issues in an effort to facilitate understanding and reconciliation of differences.

Finally, the therapist will find it difficult to maintain balance and will tend to side with one spouse when the partner appears to be acting in ignorance, egotistically or abusively. There will be a natural wish to support or even side with the apparent victim when this occurs. If the therapist errs in this way, it will only serve to exacerbate the conflict between the spouses and the therapist will loose credibility. Couples cannot feel safe with a therapist unless neutrality is maintained. If this confidence is lost, couples will feel that the therapist is judgmental and might join with their partner as therapy progresses. To prevent siding, therapists must be aware of countertransference issues as they work with both partners. They must never lose sight of the knowledge that the behavior is a reflection of pain and insecurity and not a conscious desire on the part of the partner to be unreasonable.

CMT emphasizes working with couples conjointly while being aware of the difficulties of the method. Conjoint therapy has the benefit of the following:

1. emphasizes the need for the couple to resolve problems together.
2. provides therapists with the best opportunity to assess the issues and the dynamics of the marriage

3. gives the therapist influence over the interactional patterns
4. creates a positive environment for facilitating change
5. allows an opportunity for the therapist to model appropriate behavior
6. focuses the therapists attention on the interaction and not the acting out of a particular spouse
7. minimizes transference
8. minimizes the opportunity for information to be distorted
9. reduces time needed to disseminate information.

When couples work conjointly they are constantly involved in a process which keeps reminding them that they are part of a couple and that problems and solutions to problems within the marriage are a result of what occurs between them. They therefore must take responsibility to communicate with one another to resolve differences. Often one or both spouses would strongly prefer using therapy as an opportunity to complain about their partner; "unload" their frustration to get support from the therapist or get the therapist to collaborate with them on a specific program designed to change their spouse. The partners must learn to take responsibility for their individual contribution to the problems. In most cases what is being shared can be shared with the partner present and in fact, probably already has been dysfunctionally shared (shouted) at home. With both spouses present, therapists are able to initiate treatment plans which involve both partners.

During conjoint sessions therapists are better able to accurately diagnose the problems which create the marital discord. When seen concurrently, clients present their own reality, which is always subjective and often distorted. Unless they have superhuman vision to read between the lines, how are therapists to determine what is real and what is Rashamon? In conjoint session, therapists have the advantage of comparing both views of the issue and more importantly, can observe the interactional patterns between partners.

The therapist has very little influence over the interactional patterns of couples who are being seen in concurrent therapy. Suggestions for change are ignored or distorted in the retelling. Even when the therapists' suggestions are acted upon often, they do not impact upon the marriage because the real important issues were never identified.

Observing spouses together provides therapists with a broader data base from which to draw interventions. Additionally, therapists can use numerous techniques to assist couples who are trying to change and to resolve their differences.

The importance of creating a safe and positive atmosphere for couples to examine their relationship has been articulated earlier. Seeing clients conjointly allows therapists to create such an atmosphere because the therapist can observe the patterns and issues which create the conflict and thus have more influence over what occurs. Therapists can better engage actively in using various methods to emphasize positive behaviors, to encourage growth rather than dwelling on past issues, and to model care, concern and warmth as an alternative to anger, hostility and resentment.

One of the most effective tools a therapist has to work with is the technique of modeling. By working with the conjoint method modeling can be used as a bridge building tool. We can demonstrate appropriate behavior and effective communication skills. Modeling allows for clients to see appropriate behaviors without feeling personally attacked.

A key to effective marital therapy is maintaining neutrality. Therapists can easily be lead into siding with one spouse, particularly if the couple is seen concurrently. By working with couples conjointly, therapists not only hear both sides of the issues, but also take into consideration that they will be heard by both partners. If a therapist inadvertently sides with one spouse the other will usually give them some indication that this is happening.

There is always some transference occurring in therapy, but the dynamics become more significant when the partners are seen separately. Transference is counterproductive to marital therapy, particularly when the therapist is viewed as a love object. CMTs wish to minimize transference and the conjoint method is effective in doing just that.

A major problem in seeing spouses concurrently or individually is that information can be misinterpreted and used as a weapon against the partner. The spouse seen will present a biased abridged report of the session and use it to gain control or to present a case against their partner. "He said you were too rigid!" In any case, the spouses could become further alienated. In addition, the one who is being attacked feels sided against by the therapist, which jeopardizes further conjoint sessions. Seeing clients conjointly will minimize the disinformation. Sharing information with both spouses present will also save time and repetition and possible distortion of information.

1. Working the Dyad:

The major objective in conjoint therapy is to assist couples to communicate effectively so that they will learn to negotiate issues. If this is accomplished, spouses will achieve specific goals such as the ability to problem solve and recognize and understand differences. Then they will be able to create greater autonomy within the marriage. It can be assumed that couples who come to therapy have been unable to communicate effectively, at least on some important issues, or they would not need outside assistance. It can also be assumed that the more dysfunctional the marital relationship, the poorer the communication.

Constructual marital therapists emphasize "working the dyad" or facilitating effective communication between spouses by teaching them the importance of talking with each other in an attempt to resolve discord. Couples often resist this idea as they have experienced "talking" with one another to be an experience which leads to frustration, arguments and distancing. Couples would rather talk with the therapist whom they believe will side with them, provide a cure for the problems, instruct them as to what to do, or listen sympathetically. Many therapists also prefer the idea of talking directly with individual spouses as it gives them greater control over the session and reduces the possibility for demonstrations of overt hostility. However, unless communication skills can be taught in sessions there is little hope that significant change can be made and sustained.

The first step in "working the dyad" and in aiding spouses in the art of effective communication is to observe their pattern of relating. All couples have a repetitive or circular pattern of communicating. CMT will direct couples to talk to each other about a particular issue which the therapists understand they will be unable to resolve. The therapist is not interested in the outcome of the discussion but rather in the interactional process. Once having determined the specific dysfunctional pattern, the therapist can intervene to break the circular pattern, thus allowing spouses to hear and understand each other. The things

Table II
Things Clients Do to Prevent Problem Solving

Passive Behavior
1. Withdraws (is silent)
2. Allows intrusion (passively permits distractions)
3. Procrastinates
4. Accepts guilt (takes blame whether or not appropriate)

Aggressive Behavior
5. Projects (attributes feelings and beliefs to others)
6. Attacks (threatens or is verbally abusive)
7. Blames (tries to establish that the partner is at fault)
8. Detours (changes subject)
9. Defies (challenges power figures)
10. Triangulates (brings in others)
11. Discounts (invalidates other)
12. Lectures
13. Double bind (no win)
14. Criticizes
15. Counterattacks
16. Takes non-negotiable position
17. Rejects (overt repelling of individual)
18. Accuses (statement of attack)
19. Dictates (uses power of position to win)
20. Bluffs (threatens, but backs down)
21. Minimizes (reduces significance of events, feelings)
22. Baits (invites conflict)
23. Denies (overt and verbal)
24. Becomes excessively verbal
25. Rationalizes (justifies position)
26. Floods (inundates with multiple problems)
27. Induces guilt
28. Negatively labels (using terms which will elicit anger)

Passive Aggressive Behavior
29. Cries
30. Gives double messages
31. Gives up
32. Mind reads
33. Yes, but (invalidating statement)
34. Excuses (justifies other persons behavior)
35. Doesn't accept responsibility

clients do to prevent resolving issues are predictable and are listed in Table II. Therapists must use interventions to counteract behaviors listed in the table. Once the issue is resolved, another issue is selected and the process begins again and continues until the couple can discuss and resolve problems without assistance.

Often it is difficult or impossible to work the dyad directly, therefore therapists must work indirectly by having the communication directed through them. In so doing, they might have to emphasize a role of negotiator, educator, broker or interpreter. But we recognize that these are temporary roles and that eventually the therapist wishes to be a facilitator so that the couple is able to work directly together.

B. CONCURRENT AND COMBINED THERAPY

Constructual Marital Therapists use concurrent therapy only under special circumstances and if used, efforts are made to combine this method with conjoint therapy. The two conditions which predispose to concurrent therapy are: when the couple is too reactive to be seen together and when there is a private matter which cannot be shared with the spouse. There are cases where there is so much distrust, resentment, rage and insecurity that it is impossible to prevent one or both spouses from being intrusive or verbally abusive. There are also cases where information used in the session will be used to create further conflict in the home. On the other end of the continuum, there are couples who will refuse to speak for fear of revealing themselves as they have had a history of such information having been used against them and/or they are tired of trying to be understood and accepted. In such cases, there is such a negative "we psyche" and spouses are caught so deeply in the "negative spiral" that there is little autonomy. The major objective for each partner in concurrent therapy is to work on developing sufficient autonomy and self-esteem so that the couple can begin or resume conjoint sessions.

C. COLLABORATIVE AND COMBINED COLLABORATIVE THERAPY:

Constructual marital therapists seldom use collaborative therapy and when they do it is usually in combination with conjoint therapy. There are only a few situations where it is desirable to have the spouses see separate therapists. One such case is when the therapist does not have the trust of one of the spouses. This can occur because one of the partners has been seeing a therapist for a time and the partner perceives the therapist as siding. Another situation is when one spouse wishes to work individually on ambivalence about the marriage or about a current covert affair. In such situations the therapist is in a compromising position as it is impossible to address important issues without disclosing important information which would be a betrayal of confidence. Providing separate therapists minimizes the possibility of that occurring. After individual issues have been addressed, conjoint co-therapy is then initiated.

Constructual marital therapists tend not to use combined collaborative therapy. We believe that spouses must work together to negotiate marital discord and we find combined collaborative therapy counterproductive to this effort.

D. INDIVIDUAL THERAPY

Constructual marital therapists only participate in individual therapy when one partner refuses to accept any method of therapy. In such cases, we begin by working with the cooperative spouse. Generally, efforts fail as therapists are receiving information which is one-sided. Additionally, the therapist has very little knowledge or control of the couples interactional patterns. We help the partners to recognize that very little change is possible in the relationship then let them decide if they wish to attempt to stay in a dysfunctional relationship which has little hope for change. The emphasis changes from the "we" to the "I" and from trying to influence interactional patterns to each spouse taking responsibility for finding self-fulfillment without depending on the partner. This does not suggest that the spouse must leave the marriage, but that each must accept the reality of the relationship's limitations if it is to continue.

E. SUMMARY

In conclusion, constructual marital therapists have decided that the most successful method of therapy is conjoint therapy. This method helps to develop the communication skills necessary to achieve a harmonious marriage. Under special circumstances we use combined or conjoint/collaborative therapy. Combined/collaborative is not used, but individual therapy is provided when one spouse refuses treatment.

12

CONSTRUCTUAL MARITAL THERAPY PARADIGMS

A MAJOR INNOVATIVE FEATURE of Constructual Marital Therapy is that it provides five rather than the standard two paradigms customarily used in the treatment of troubled marriages. In addition to the traditional approaches of marital therapy and divorce therapy, constructual marital therapists add to their repertoire the additional choices of individuation, accommodation and veritive therapies. Diagram IV illustrates how these five paradigms are interconnected.

A. INITIAL INTERVIEW

Treatment begins in the initial interview during which the therapist conducts a very structured and organized session in order to assess the needs of the couple and to establish together with them a treatment plan designed to meet those needs. It is desirable that both partners attend this session. This will avoid repeating questions in order to gain factual knowledge. Further, with both partners in attendance, the therapist can begin to demonstrate to them that they must work together in order to resolve issues. Additionally, if a spouse enters later in therapy he/she might be defensive, believing that the spouse already engaged in therapy has presented a convincing indictment of him/her and that the therapist has already sided with the spouse. Finally, the therapist is in the position of assessing information from both partners and is more able to understand the dynamics of interaction within the marriage.

Diagram IV
Types of Couple Therapy

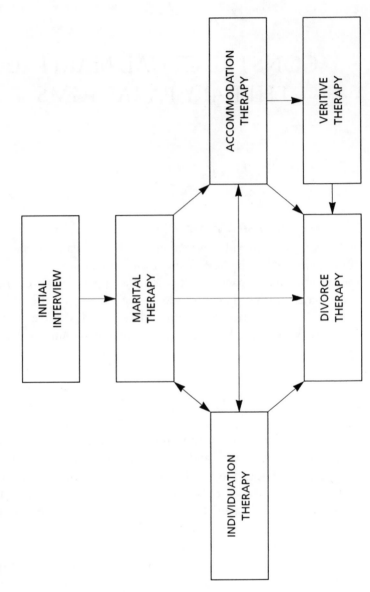

The interview begins with the Socialization stage.[16] Here the therapist joins with the couple in a warm and friendly manner while he/she obtains general background information. The primary goal of this stage is to create a positive and comfortable atmosphere. This will minimize resistance between the couple and the therapist. The second goal of this stage is to acquire knowledge about each of the partner's individual characteristics and to watch how they relate to each other. The third goal is to obtain a cursory understanding about the couple's current and past relationship and social situation. Questions during the socialization stage include:

1. Do you have children? (If yes, how many and what age?)
2. Are you both employed? (At what job or profession and for how long?)
3. Does anyone except your children live with you?
4. Where do you live? How long at this address?
5. What individual interests do each of you have?
6. Do you (both of you) enjoy your work?
7. Do your in-laws live close by?
8. Do you have strong religious beliefs? (Are you religiously active? Do you share these beliefs?)

After obtaining background information the therapists takes a prior history of the marriage. Each partner is allowed to express his/her view and the therapist maintains balance by not allowing the session to be dominated by either of the spouses. In this phase we ask such questions as:

1. How long have you been married?
2. What were your ages when you married?
3. Were your parents pleased by the marriage?
4. Before marriage, how long did you know one another and under what circumstances?
5. Did you live together before marriage? (How long?)
6. Did you marry primarily out of "love" or "convenience"?
7. What was your marriage like at the start? How has it changed?
8. How would you each describe the current status of your marriage?
9. When did the major problems in your marriage begin?

If there is a previous history of marriage, it is important to obtain a brief history of the former marriage(s). Critical questions are: did the current partners know each other while one or both were previously married, if yes, what was their relationship during this time? How soon did the couple start dating and how soon after the divorce or death of a previous spouse did they marry? This information helps the therapist assess whether there was enough time for the spouse(s) to complete a differentiation process and to mourn the loss of the earlier relationship.

During the second, or "problem" stage of the interview, the therapist asks each partner to define his/her perception of the problems and to reveal how long the problems have existed and what they have done in an effort to resolve them. During this stage the therapist does not allow either spouse to give a "dissertation" on the problems, but rather tries to elicit succinct responses. At this point the therapist does not want to encourage a discussion of issues. The therapist's primary interest is to understand each partner's view of the issues, discern the severity of the marital problems and determine the level of agreement between the spouses.

In the third, or "interactional" stage, spouses are asked to select a problem and attempt to resolve it. During this process the therapist is able to assess the communication pattern of the marriage, the ability of the spouses to problem solve and the degree of reactiveness the couple manifests. The therapist allows no more than ten to fifteen minutes for the couple to discuss the problem.

During the fourth, or "expectation" stage of the interview, spouses are asked why they decided to come to therapy. Some couples will state that they came because they believe it will be helpful. Others will admit that they were forced to come by their partner. Some couples cannot articulate a clear reason for coming. The clients are then asked what determined this timing—that is what is happening now that compelled them to make this decision. Most come out of desperation and frustration. Often they are dealing with an important crisis. In many of these cases one of the partners is threatening to end the relationship. The therapist asks them if they feel that separation or divorce would be a possible solution to their problems. This allows the therapist to determine if the couple feels "trapped" in the marriage and to assess the boundaries in which he/she will be able to work.

The next set of questions relate to spousal expectations from the therapist and from the therapeutic process. Couples will often have unrealistic expectations. They perceive the therapist as someone who will solve their problems and/or act as a judge. The therapist must correct such preconceptions.

During this phase of therapy the couple is briefly seen separately and each is asked if they are romantically involved with another person. If there is a current affair, the participant is asked if the spouse knows about the other person and what the affair means to the participant in terms of commitment and involvement. If the affair is secret, the therapist must determine whether or not to continue treatment.

The second and only other question we ask the couple while seen separately is to evaluate the degree to which they love their spouse on an ascending scale from zero to ten. They are asked to use their own definition of love and to describe to us their understanding of that word. Their responses are a good indication level of the spouse's emotional commitment to the marriage.

During the fifth, or "information" stage of the interview, the therapist, cognizant of the five reasons couples have problems, explains to the couple his/her understanding of why marriages develop conflicts. He/she also explains which of the five areas of difficulty applies to their problem(s). The therapist then explains his/her basic assumptions about marriage, including the belief that marriage is a process of integration— that is taking two lives and attempting to develop one smooth working relationship. The therapist might discuss the problems which develop from basing a marriage on unrealistic self-centered expectations rather than a mature giving of self. The therapist will discuss the need for reciprocity and responsibility in the relationship.

During this stage the therapist will explain to the couple the need to develop an enhancing relationship. The idea of the covenant relationship will be introduced and all the stages of marital development described. The therapist will explain to the couple the need for them to both understand each other and themselves, the need to accept differences and the importance of effective communication.

The therapist will conclude the fifth stage by explaining to the couple what they can and cannot expect from therapy and what will be required of the couple if they continue. It will be made clear to the couple that the therapist cannot "save" marriages and that there are no magical cures. What they can expect from therapy is an approach which will allow them to see each other and themselves more clearly, learn effective communication skills, help recognize real feelings and defense responses, and receive training in problem solving. They will also learn that therapy is a conduit for change in marriage and that change requires commitment, time and energy. Homework assignments will be explained as the couple learn they are beginning a process which must continue not only after they leave the therapist's office, but after they leave therapy. Ideally, sessions are taped and the tape given to the couple to review before the next session.

In the sixth, or "summation" stage of the session, couples are asked if they wish to continue therapy and if they do, the first homework assignment is given. The assignment is to be done separately and not shared until the next session. Each spouse is asked to list twenty-five one word adjectives about him/herself and twenty-five adjectives about his/her partner—to list five things desired from the marriage and to list five things he/she can do to help the marriage. The homework assignment is designed to create some autonomy, help spouses assess themselves and their partners, encourage partners to recognize their contribution toward marital discord, assess the partners willingness to assume responsibility for conflict, assist couples to define for themselves their marital expectations, and obtain informational building blocks to help the couple "build bridges" in their marriage.

After the assignment is given, the therapist explains that they will begin problem solving in the next session. Regular meeting times are established, policy on cancelled or broken appointments explained and the payment of fees clarified.

If the initial interview is well managed, the therapist should come out of it with a wealth of information. Among other important facts, he/she should know:

1. Under what circumstances the marriage began
2. The spouses perceptions of the marital problems
3. If the issues are situational, transitional or chronic
4. The initial casual conflicts and the pattern of perpetuation and escalation of problems

5. The impact of past and present living conditions
6. If past relationship issues are affecting this marriage
7. Individual communication levels
8. The circular pattern of communication the couple has established
9. What the couple expects from therapy
10. The stage of marital development the couple has reached.
11. To what degree is the couple caught in the negative spiral.

The therapist can now determine which paradigm will be most useful and, within that paradigm, which method of treatment be most helpful in the initial phase of therapy.

B. MARITAL THERAPY

Some couples seek marital therapy when they are unable to resolve a situational crisis or transitional problem and they see that it could evolve into something more serious. In most cases however, couples are locked into the negotiation stage of marriage and cannot resolve chronic problems. If they cannot transcend this stage of marriage the unresolved issues create continuous conflict, critical behavior and emotional distancing.

Couples usually enter therapy only after they reluctantly realize that they need professional help after trying, usually at a great emotional price, to solve their own problems. They trust that the therapist will be able to understand them, teach them to resolve differences and help them to develop skills necessary for an enhancing marriage. No matter how conflictual or unhappy the marriage, the couples we see in Marital Therapy are the ones who are seeking to establish or maintain a relationship that is supportive, caring and nurturing. The purpose of Marital Therapy, then, is to guide couples through the stages of marriage toward a covenant relationship.

They may come into therapy with one or many problems. They may or may not be in agreement about what is causing the marital discord. They will all have unique problems and relationship dynamics

—but the presenting problem will include one or more of the following factors:

1. Little or no effective communication
2. An inability to accommodate differences
3. Disagreement about child rearing practices
4. An inability to develop an enhancing sexual relationship
5. An inability or unwillingness to understand one another
6. Little or no trust
7. No development of common interests
8. Financial issues
9. The conviction that it is the spouse who must change
10. Feelings of betrayal if there has been infidelity

It has been the experience of this therapist that resolution of the presented conflict(s) is seldom the determining factor in whether couples fulfill their potential for a happy marriage. I believe the determining factors to be: whether the couple feels free to end the marriage, the degree of dependency need and the depth of the loving feelings of both partners. When couples have fully internalized the fact that they do not love or are not loved by their partner they will end the marriage, even if there is little or no conflict. Most people will not endure a marriage without mutual love. However couples will stay in a loveless marriage when they do not feel free to end it. There are couples who are not free to end a marriage because of religious or cultural mandates. People will also stay together in loveless relationships out of neediness. In these marriages often the only feeling is mutual hatred, but the marriage plods on because of physical or emotional dependency. The greater the dependency, the more likely spouses will try to maintain the marriage. A marriage with no love seldom grows without assistance beyond the accommodation stage. Couples in such marriages generally find the relationship unfulfilling and invest most of their emotional energy in other interests or in their children.

The couple might have been living with their problems for years or they might have been catapulted into therapy by one overwhelming crisis. In most cases, the problems themselves are only symptomatic of a deeper conflict. But Constructual Marital Therapists must begin by addressing themselves to the identified problem. It is possible to simultaneously address the underlying problem(s)—to look for the termites in the cellar—in order to create a solid foundation on which to build.

Table III lists ten goals of marital therapy and addresses both presenting and underlying problems.

Table III
Ten Goals of Marital Therapy

1. IMPROVE COMMUNICATION SKILLS so that the couple can articulate feelings, needs, expectations, and problems in a manner that increases the likelihood of correct perception and appropriate response. This includes focusing on both verbal and non-verbal elements, semantics, and tonal qualities.

2. ASSIST CLIENTS IN UNDERSTANDING THEMSELVES AND SPOUSE so that these insights can be used to facilitate both the recognition and resolution of problems and the identification of commonalities that can strengthen relationships.

3. ASSIST CLIENTS IN RECOGNIZING AND ACCEPTING OR ACCOMMO-DATING DIFFERENCES in order to reduce conflict over non-negotiable issues, values, and expectations.

4. HELP TO CREATE AUTONOMY FOR EACH SPOUSE so that they can function from a position of equal strength and reciprocal concern within the marital arena.

5. ASSIST COUPLES IN RECOGNIZING INDIVIDUAL ISSUES THAT ARE BEING PROJECTED INTO THE CURRENT RELATIONSHIP so that they can resolve these personal issues or elect to block their intrusion into the marital arena. These may include personal intra-psychic problems, unresolved problems related to family of origin, or past relationships.

6. ASSIST COUPLES IN UNDERSTANDING THE DYNAMICS WHICH UNDERLIE THEIR CURRENT PROBLEMS in order to clarify the forces which contribute to their conflict and to facilitate the identification of behaviors that can modify these dysfunctions.

7. ASSIST CLIENTS TO DEFINE, UNDERSTAND, AND NEGOTIATE CURRENT EXPECTATIONS AND GOALS IN THE RELATIONSHIP in order to develop an organized, systematic approach to problem resolution.

8. ASSIST CLIENTS TO MOVE FROM NON-NEGOTIABLE ISSUES TO NEGOTIABLE ONES in order to end blind alley conflict.

9. IMPROVE PROBLEM SOLVING SKILLS so that clients can learn to effectively understand, accept, and resolve their differences.

10. ASSIST SPOUSES IN MOVING FROM AN INTERACTIONAL PATTERN OF CONTROL TO ONE OF GIVING because spouses who give allow for autonomy and flexibility in a relationship.

In summary, the purpose of Marital Therapy is to assist couples in conflict to resolve differences so that an enhancing marriage can be achieved. The therapist must begin with the presenting problems, but must also take into consideration important individual and marital issues. Some couples will decide, during the course of Marital Therapy, that they do not love each other and they will thus seek a divorce or learn to accept an accommodating marriage.

C. INDIVIDUATION THERAPY

There are often times during the course of therapy when the therapists find that they are not able to help couples to communicate effectively. Numerous intervention are made but the results are the same—spouses continue to blame their partners for the problems, attack each others thoughts, feelings and beliefs, act defensively when constructive criticism is offered, attempt to win rather than negotiate disagreements and refuse to try anything different to improve the relationship. In sort, little or no change takes place. In such cases, it is not unusual for therapists to conclude that there are irreconcilable differences and to offer divorce therapy. However, in such situations individuation, accommodation or veritive therapy might be viable options to facilitate positive change.

The couple might be unable to resolve differences because there are personal issues which need to be addressed before change can occur. In such cases individuation therapy is the paradigm of choice.

In individuation therapy, each partner works directly with the therapist in an effort to address the idiosyncratic feelings, beliefs, concerns and behaviors which get in the way of effective communication. The problems might have been brought into but been made worse by the marriage, presented themselves during the marriage, or even been created by the marital dyad. In any case, working the dyad is not yet possible as one partner cannot influence the resolution of the issues affecting the actions and feelings of the other spouse, one spouse cannot accept help from his/her partner or a partner cannot be helpful or supportive. The inability of the couple to work in harmony is the result of one or more of the following factors: ambivalence about remaining in the marriage; individual insecurities negate trust, respect and/or love; there are non-negotiable demands for change.

By working directly with the therapist, the spouses will be given an opportunity to: resolve an issue irrespective of the partner's view of the problem; work on an individual problem; or consider the possibility of making changes required by the partner.

Marital issues requiring independent decision making related to ambivalence can be divided into the following five categories:

1. Decisions about continuing the marriage
2. Inability to initiate a desired divorce/separation
3. Deciding whether feelings of love are present
4. Deciding if it is possible to accept differences
5. Deciding if it is possible to establish or regain trust.

Until these issues are clearly resolved the therapist does not know if marital therapy can be continued or if accommodation, veritive or divorce therapy would be the most effective choice.

Often when marital therapy begins one or both of the partners feels ambivalent about continuing the marriage. The ambivalence can be due to a variety of reasons. One partner could be involved in an affair. Some spouses come to believe over the years that the marriage was based on convenience and not love. In some couples there are still feelings of love, but these feelings are lost in a haze of conflictual behaviors and reactions. Many couples have been caught in the negative spiral and are already emotionally divorced. In any case, the ambivalent feelings prevail and prevent partners from making a clear decision about the marriage.

Therapists are sometimes faced with a case in which one partner is definite about wanting a divorce and the other wants to continue the marriage. In such cases, the partner who wishes to end the marriage would like his/her partner to cooperate to make the action less painful. The partner who wishes to continue the marriage either still feels love for the spouse, is dependent on the spouse and/or believes that if they work together the marriage is still salvageable. It is common, in such cases, for each partner to come to therapy to try to gain a strong advocate for his/her position. The therapist must be careful not to side or the partner who feels negated will generally withdraw from treatment to seek support elsewhere.

There are times when the couple is overtly there for marital therapy but one partner has already made a secret decision to end the marriage. The abandoning spouse wants support from the therapist as he/she is afraid to initiate divorce proceedings. In such cases, the first thing the therapist must decide is whether he/she will conspire with this partner as it is clear that the other spouse is trusting the therapist to focus on enhancing the marriage. If the therapist believes that it is unethical and/or unhelpful to withhold important information he/she must require that honesty be established before therapy can proceed.

We will not address the myriad reasons that lead to a married person's painful suspicion that among all the feelings they have about their partner, there is a conspicuous absence of the feeling of love. However, the marriage cannot move until this suspicion is confirmed or proven wrong. Nothing their partner can say or do will answer this question. The questioning partner must determine the answer alone. The relationship can continue in the absence of love, but both partners must know and accept that this is the status of the relationship.

Couples often spend years trying to metamorphosize each other into a more accurate version of their ideal mate. These unresolved and desperate mating dances only leave them frustrated and exhausted. During the course of marital therapy, the partners are taught new steps that lead them to appreciate the intricate nuances of the dance and accept that they cannot make major changes in their partner's performance. They must accommodate, keep dancing in circles, or move on.

This therapist believes that trust is second only to love in those qualities which are intrinsic to a good marriage. Without trust it is difficult to validate love and to sustain feelings of commitment, honesty, security and caring. Whatever the reason for the lack of trust, a marriage infected with it is often firmly enmeshed in the negative spiral. Without deep feeling of trust, partners not only become reactive but turn to such destructive behavior as "mind reading" an insidious process which leads to such devaluating statements as: "I don't care what you say, I know what you mean!" and "You say you care about . . . but I know what you are really thinking."

The inability to trust ones' partner aborts any attempts to accept differences, resolve disagreements and correct misconceptions. Once trust is lost, the partners must decide if it can be rekindled. It has been the experience of this therapist that when trust is totally lost, love is also lost and there is little hope for an enhancing marriage and in fact most such marriages will end in divorce.

Problems which interfere with the building of a successful marriage are not always limited to relationship dynamics or interactional patterns. Often problems arise out of personal insecurities or a specific conflictual issue. These factors include: poor self-esteem, specific fears such as jealousy or phobias, poor impulse control, unresolved family of origin problems or unresolved problems with former spouses. Individuation therapy is vital for the definition and resolution of such problems so that a path toward a successful marriage can be cleared.

There are cases where one partner demands specific attitude or behavioral changes before agreeing to participate in marital therapy. Some spouses will assume no responsibility for contributing to any problems of the marriage and insist that their partner must make all the changes. The accused partners often acquiesce to the demands because they are driven to maintain the relationship at all costs. When this interaction develops, that is one partner forcing the other to make all the concessions and assume all the responsibility, an emotional divorce is inevitable and the end of the relationship is usually in progress.

Individuation therapy is not individual psychotherapy. Although the emphasis of the therapy has changed from the "we" to the "I," constructual marital therapists are always cognizant of the relationship as a whole. There is the constant realization that this is a process where individual growth is tied to the growth of the marital relationship. The focus is on attempting to help spouses recognize how their personal issues influence the marriage. An example of this is a case where a therapist, while working with a wife who had unresolved conflicts with her father, helped the woman to recognize how those issues were being projected onto her husband.

As constructual marital therapists are continuously treating the marriage, even when individual problems are being addressed, most individuation therapy is conducted in conjoint sessions. The contradictions for conjoint therapy were previously discussed.

Conjoint sessions remind couples of their interconnectedness by the simple fact that they are in the room together. It is also helpful that when a spouse is revealing him/herself to the therapist, the partner is a silent witness to the interaction. Not only will the therapist be able to observe the reactions of the observing spouse and to gain additional information, but the partners will gain new insights, both by what is revealed and by how the therapist handles the interaction. Such insight will often lead to positive change in the relationship. Finally, the conjoint session allows the observing spouse an opportunity to show supportive behavior and it allows the therapist the possibility of gaining assistance in therapy assignments. For example, after seeing her husband's anguish over the death of his mother, a wife was easily encouraged to accompany him to his mother's grave to support him as he grieved his loss. Thus, unlike concurrent therapy, which by its very structure encourages separateness, conjoint sessions maximize the opportunities for spouses to grow together.

Although couples will always present new issues and unique problems, the following ten goals listed in Table IV should be kept in mind when doing individuation therapy.

Individuation therapy allows constructual marital therapists to select from any number of treatment modalities to diagnose and treat particular problems. For example, the therapist could use strategic interventions to help a phobic client, the work of Kübler-Ross to help with issues of grief, or some of the concepts presented in Contextual Family Therapy to address family of origin problems. A client might need only one session or might require several months to complete individuation therapy. In any case, when the work is completed, a decision can then be made to continue with marital or move to accommodation, veritive or divorce therapy. If both spouses are in individuation therapy, marital therapy should not begin until both have resolved their issues or problems. However, highly skilled therapists might be able to combine individuation with other paradigms.

Table IV
Ten Goals of Individuation Therapy
1. Assist partners in defining issues or problems which prevent them from working together for problem resolution.
2. Assist partners in developing a treatment focus, including the selection of the method of treatment.
3. Assist partners in achieving the objectives articulated in the treatment plan.
4. Assist spouses in maintaining and recognizing their interconnectedness (unless they elect to end the marriage).
5. Provide information to assist with problem resolution.
6. Assist spouses in recognizing and taking responsibility for the dynamics which influence their behaviors.
7. Assist spouses in being aware of their own feelings, particularly those that impact on behavior.
8. Assist spouses in recognizing their own strengths and ability to control their future.
9. Assist spouses in being autonomous so that dignity can be fully realized.
10. Assist spouses in being assertive so that they can behave in a way that reinforces their autonomy.

D. ACCOMMODATION THERAPY

> She fears him and will always ask
> What fated her to choose him;
> She meets in his engaging mask
> All reasons to refuse him;
> But what she meets and what she fears
> Are less than are the downward years, . . .
> Of age, where she to lose him. . .[17]
>
> *Eros Turrannos*
> — *Edwin Arlington Robinson*

There are marriages that endure for years in the absence of love. We will call these relationship "accommodating marriages." The "tie that binds" could be the bond of children, religion, culture, family, or physical, financial and/or emotional dependency. It is possible for such marriages to reach the integration phase of marital development. Individual autonomy can be maintained and a supportive, enhancing mutual friendship is possible. Personal and family goals can be set and achieved and common interests can be shared.

Accommodating marriages can be satisfying and fulfilling. In order to achieve a successful accommodating marriage, couples need to be mature, sensitive, caring, respectful of their partner's needs and accepting of the limitations of the relationship. When these qualities and conditions are not present in the relationship conflict is likely.

Therapists often observe marriages where there is clearly no love and yet the marriage continues in the face of constant conflict and even overt hostility. Divorce is not an option in some of these cases. The therapist knows that marital therapy will not be helpful and that divorce therapy will be rejected. In such situation accommodation therapy can be offered to couples to help them to maximize the potential for the development of a harmonious relationship. This paradigm is not often used as most couples believe that they cannot continue a relationship in which there is no love. If the therapist knows that the marriage is destined to continue even though conflict is apparent and there is little or no love, accommodation therapy is a viable alternative therapeutic approach which will help the couple resolve conflicts and accept differences.

It might seem that one or both of the spouses would have to be psychologically insecure to remain in a loveless marriage and this is often the case. One client gave me this amazing reason for staying in his marriage: "I invested years in helping her become successful—if I am going to be miserable, she is going to be miserable with me because I'm not going to let her find happiness with someone else." Should this marriage be saved? That is not the decision of a therapist. All we can do, if the couple is determined to stay together, is help the couple make the relationship a comfortable one, free as possible from conflict and overt expressions of hostility.

In many cases a marriage remains intact because of such pragmatic reasons as providing a secure home for the children, wanting to continue a satisfactory sexual relationship instead of entering the dangerous world of single life, or sharing a successful business partnership. The reasons might have nothing to do with poor self-esteem or emotional insecurity as many romantics and/or mental health professionals would like to believe.

When these couples begin therapy they are often aware at some level that they are trying to perpetuate a loveless relationship, but they have not internalized or accepted that fact. Even when there is no love, there is often an expectation of love and this leads to a constant frustrating battle over the affirmation of feelings that do not exist. One husband, for example, admitted that he hated his wife but yet he was disappointed and angered when she was not lovingly solicitous and attentive to him when he had the flu. Often such couples have been caught in the negative spiral for years and are emotionally divorced.

Accommodation therapy is often a long and difficult process when the spouses have lost fundamental trust. There are strong feelings of resentment and a fear of being emotionally injured. There are often strong dependency needs and differentiation is minimal. Normally, concurrent individuation is necessary to assist spouses to regain self-esteem and autonomy and to accept their personal contribution toward the marital discord. The following are goals designed for constructual marital therapists engaged in accommodation therapy.

The first goal of accommodation therapy is to help couples learn to stop blaming the other for the unhappiness in the marriage and instead assume responsibility. It must be made clear that responsibility does not imply fault or that either partner is bad, stupid or malicious. The couple must come to see that the marriage, as it stands, is destructive and that there is the potential for much more happiness, harmony and fulfillment than presently exists.

The second goal is to assist each partner in recognizing the truth about the relationship and the foundation on which it is based. This means accepting the painful reality that there is either no love or there is unrequited love, the marriage will not be based on shared love and signs of love cannot be expected. The reasons that love does not exist will have to be examined, understood and accepted. It is difficult and painful for couples to accept the idea that their marriage is not founded on love, but if one or both do not accept the reality of the marriage, they will be constantly slipping back into dysfunctional patterns and emotional demands. The goal of the therapist is to help the couple to internalize that their's is a marriage of accommodation and that such marriages are workable. Often the therapist must help the spouses experience and work through primary feelings of loss, failure and emptiness. The therapist will often have to assist in helping the clients to grieve both the death of the love in the marriage and the death of the hope of love in the marriage.

If the couple is able to accept the truth of the relationship, the therapeutic goal is to help the couple give up unrealistic expectations. The couple must learn the simple but painful truth that loving feelings cannot be shared if they do not exist. During this process, the therapist will assist couples in the recognition and development of realistic expectations for the marriage. As previously indicated, what can be expected is a peaceful, satisfying and somewhat fulfilling relationship. Finally, the goal of therapy is to assist spouses in finding alternatives for positive interactions in their life. There is an emphasis on developing social, educational, recreational, artistic or political interests outside the marriage.

In summary, accommodation therapy is provided to couples in conflict who do not have a marriage based on mutual love but who are determined to stay together. Accommodation therapy helps couples in such a relationship to recognize and accept the current conditions of the marriage and so establish realistic expectations for meeting their needs and living in harmony. If accomplished successfully, this kind of marriage can be quite rewarding.

E. VERITIVE THERAPY

Veritive therapy is a transitional therapeutic plan designed to illuminate the crossroads of decision making. Its purpose is to help the couple to recognize the truth of their relationship. In order to establish a successful accommodating marriage—one in which there is peace, mutual respect and minimal courtesy, both spouses must consent to the arrangement and recognize its limitations. But there are many cases where maintaining a marriage which has been recognized to be loveless is not acceptable or all attempts to develop such a relationship have failed. In some cases, one of the partners is willing to accept an accommodating marriage and the other is not. A real dilemma occurs when divorce is not considered a possibility because of religious, cultural or practical considerations and yet one or both of the partners feel they cannot continue in the marriage because of profound distrust, resentment, or a belief that a satisfactory marriage cannot exist without love.

When efforts at individuation and accommodation therapy have failed to help couples find a peaceful solution to a marriage without mutual love, the therapist has no other option but to offer veritive therapy.

The truth of such relationship can be intolerably painful to accept. Although in some cases reality will lead to a decision to learn to trust and forgive their spouse for past conflicts, most such couples will choose to live in a conflictual, frustrating and pleasureless relationship. There are couples for whom the truth is that they do not share love. Others will have to learn to accept that their spouse will always be rigid, unsupporting, uncaring, insensitive and/or verbally or physically abusing. When faced with the reality of their relationship, a few spouses will be jolted into contemplating divorce as an option for their situation. The ensuing dilemma of having to choose between unpleasant alternatives can be helped, in some cases, with individuation therapy. However, most couples who have reached this stage of therapy will continue in their unhappy and conflictual relationships. When couples have accepted the unfortunate, unchangeable truth of their relationship and make a firm decision to remain in their conflictual marriage, treatment is terminated.

Constructual marital therapists have established specific goals for Veritive Therapy. Initially, the therapist must provide support and understanding to their clients who generally begin to experience great pain in the recognition of the hopelessness of their situation. Spouses begin to see that they cannot change and that the relationship cannot change. Therapists must support their clients' rights to self-determination, even their right to remain in a destructive marriage. They should help clients to recognize the reality of their marital situation; i.e., a marriage which is not, and never will be, enhancing, fulfilling or satisfying. Finally, therapists should assist clients in accepting their own contribution to maintaining an unhappy marriage, even if that contribution is simply the fact that they are allowing the relationship to continue.

Spouses who will not consider a divorce or accept the reality of an accommodation marriage will generally withdraw from therapy. To continue in therapy would be an attack on their denial system. They do not wish to be reminded of the hopelessness of their situation, they also do not want to accept responsibility for their actions. Often the therapist is left with one spouse who is willing to accept an accommo- dating marriage—with no cooperation from the partner. It is unusual for one spouse to have the power to engage the partner in making the necessary changes to bring about an accommodating marriage. The therapy will often end with the client feeling hopeless about the marital situation.

I suspect that life situations strongly influence the future of such relationships. I recall Mr. and Mrs. O., who terminated therapy after one year and who firmly believed that they would spend the rest of their lives being unhappy together. A follow up interview revealed that Mrs. O. had subsequently become involved in a clandestine love affair. About that time Mr. O. had made a decision to make a career move to another city. She chose to stay behind for awhile, hoping the affair would develop into a committed relationship. The affair ended, but when Mrs. O. decided to return to her husband, he told her he wished to initiate a divorce. The separation had given Mr. O. enough time to individuate from his wife and the reasons he had felt for continuing the marriage were no longer important.

In summary, Veritive Therapy is necessary for spouses who are not willing to contemplate divorce or to accept an accommodation marriage. Emphasis is on assisting the couple to recognize the truth, or reality of their situation. In most cases, the couple will leave therapy and continue to be unhappy in their marriage. It is then up to situational events to influence any chance for change in the future.

F. DIVORCE THERAPY

It is a myth that when couples divorce it is usually because one or both is selfish or self-centered and it is easier to end a conflictual rela- tionship than it is to remain in the marriage and attempt to work out the problems. There are few life experiences more painful than divorce, even for couples who have been unhappy and combative for years.

When a couple divorces, they not only give up a primary relation-ship, but they give up all mutual dreams, hopes and plans. The present is always radically altered. They will often find themselves in a new place, with half of their possessions, and with the "we psyche" suddenly severed, feeling very much like half a person. Often friends and relatives, trying not to side, will simply back off and leave the divorcing person completely alone at a time when loneliness looms large in empty rooms. If children are involved, the situation becomes more complex.

Not only is the present altered, but divorce alters the past. Memories become painful, joyful holidays, romantic weekends—all the good that was shared, is suddenly remembered. A simple snapshot of a casual pleasant picnic will be a devastating *momento mori*. It feels as if there has been a death in the family but no one was buried. At this stage there develops what I will call a "ghost marriage." The specter of what once was and, if it is allowed to remain unburied, what will always be: a shadow lurking in the background ready to criticize, condemn and judge.

LXIX

One need not be a chamber to be haunted
One need not be a house;
the brain has corridors surpassing
Material place

Far safer, of a midnight meeting
External ghost
Than an interior confronting
that whiter host. . .[18]

— *Emily Dickinson*

The purpose of divorce therapy is to provide emotional support to clients and to help them work through this painful transition in a way that will be least damaging to everyone in the family. Couples who continue to battle their way through the divorce process physically separate from their partners but remain emotionally stuck in the rela-tionship. They are not free, but they carry with them the emotional baggage of insecurity, unresolved issues, anger and fear. And there is seldom anyone who will help carry this kind of baggage. Friends withdraw from what they perceive is self-inflicted pain. Families often offer unwelcome criticism of the spouse or simplistic advice. The clients themselves must learn to integrate the good and bad, after the clouds of anger and resentment clear, and to rebuild a single house on a strong foundation. Autonomy must be regained and reinforced before the new house is strong enough to take in a new partner.

Divorce therapy is often a very intense experience both for the clients and the therapist. In some cases, the clients come to therapy having resolved most of the issues and want some support in ending the marriage as peacefully as possible. Even in these cases, sessions can be very intense as the clients will express the deep pain associated with grieving the loss of the relationship and all the unfulfilled expectations, dreams and plans. In most divorce cases, however, couples are still locked in the paradoxical position of a "we psyche" and a negative spiral. There are feelings of the loss of dignity and the loss of self-esteem. Blaming is common and conflicts continue to erupt over unmet needs. Even spouses who have been emotionally divorced for years will often fight the reality of an actual divorce. When the decision is finally made to proceed with a divorce, each spouse is motivated to blame the other for the failure of the marriage and to express anger at being victimized. In the initial phases of Divorce Therapy the therapist will often feel like a referee.

When only one spouse wants the divorce, the conflict is intensified. This can be an agonizing process for both spouses as the pleas and promises of the renounced spouse are repeatedly rejected. There are cases where a divorcing client who was the victim of physical abuse during the marriage is threatened with violence if a divorce is pursued. Finally, because autonomy is so mitigated and pain and fear so intense, some clients will threaten suicide if a divorce is initiated. The burden of such threats is incalculable. I know of a tragic case where, after a separation, an estranged husband killed himself on his wife's birthday. It took years of therapy for the widow to deal with her feelings of guilt and anger.

Divorce Therapy is stressful for the therapist as well as the clients. There are clients who will desperately beg for help in keeping a doomed marriage together. Rather than blame themselves or their spouse, the therapist is often chosen as an appropriate villain for not saving the marriage. I have had colleagues who were threatened with lawsuits or even with physical violence for their perceived role in encouraging a divorce. One enraged husband threatened a colleague of mine with a gun in an attempt to get his estranged wife's address from the therapist. All threats of suicide and homicide must, of course, be taken seriously. While we cannot accurately predict behavior, if a divorce ends tragically it will help us to know that we did everything in our power: i.e., provided support, encouraged hospitalization, and warned principals. But there are times when we cannot anticipate violence and enraged spouses are especially unpredictable in behavior. We can only make use of our best instincts and training and usually that will allow us to make appropriate decisions. There are clients who are determined to kill themselves rather than be divorced. We do not always know in advance who they are.

Divorce is not simply the physical separation of two people. In most cases it includes:

1. emotional separation
2. redefinition of autonomy for both
3. regaining self-esteem and dignity
4. child custody arrangements
5. dealing with the emotional needs of children
6. settlement of finances and property
7. redefining relationships with friends
8. redefining relationships with in-laws
9. changes in living arrangements
10. handling changes in social life
11. meeting religious or cultural expectations

Variables which will influence how couples will respond to divorce include:

1. psychological maturity of spouses
2. length of marriage
3. age and number of children
4. financial and physical independence

5. family and social support
6. tightness of negative spiral
7. agreement about the decision to divorce
8. religious beliefs and cultural expectations
9. conditions under which the marriage began

There are several paradigms from which to select that will provide a background for understanding the process of divorce. These paradigms address the important issues and the stages of the divorce process. I find Kessler's Seven Stages of Divorce useful in treating divorcing clients.[19] These are:

1. disillusionment
2. erosion
3. detachment
4. physical separation
5. mourning
6. second adolescence
7. hard work

According to Kessler, divorce begins when one or both of the spouses becomes seriously disillusioned about the marriage, questioning at a profound level; whether they made a mistake in marrying, if they ever loved their partner, or has the love they once felt ended. These issues might remain on a preconscious level for a long time as spouses are afraid to face the consequences of negative answers to these important questions. This would lead to such considerations as: "Am I willing to initiate and take responsibility for a divorce?" Instead of addressing the dissolutionment directly, the relationship will begin to erode as efforts toward an enhancing relationship end. Instead, spouses invest themselves in other activities such as developing a career, social, athletic or political activities, or increased energy in child rearing.

With many couples, erosion begins with verbal conflicts which eventually leads to a tightening negative spiral. As a result there is an increasing loss of affinity and an eventual emotional divorce. Detachment follows at which time the feelings of abandonment, loneliness and hopelessness begin to grow into a hollow feeling of great emptiness.

The emotional pain increases to the point where major surgery, the complete severing of the relationship, is the one hope of saving both partners in the conjoint psyche. The separation will only be successful if each partner has the potential to develop into a complete person.

It is not unusual for one or both spouses to become emotionally involved with another person as the reality of an impending divorce becomes internalized. This will help to cope with the pain of feeling rejected and unloved and affords an opportunity to express loving feelings. An affair will contribute to the erosion and detachment taking place in the marriage. For some, a lover will make it easier to make a decision about the marriage because there will be a source of support and nurturance and for others there is already a commitment to a new marital relationship. In any case, this therapist believes that in most cases involvement in a significant loving relationship shortly following a divorce will serve to short circuit the mourning process—a stage that is vital for individuals to differentiate and develop autonomy. As a result, insecurities, unresolved issues and painful feelings are carried into new relationships.

I believe that the uncompleted mourning of a marriage is one of the most important reasons that the divorce rate in second marriages is so high. Because the ghosts of the first marriage have not been buried, remarried couples are often dealing with two or more marriages as they try to negotiate a new life.

Once the couple has separated the process of mourning the loss of the marriage can begin. Individuals will experience feelings of anger, betrayal, rage, fear, helplessness, inadequacy and loneliness. Some will become disoriented or even suicidal. For some, the emotional pain is so great that they have the desire to, or do in fact return to their partner. The pain of separation is great and in some cases medication will help or another relationship provide balm, but the only real cure is realizing that this is part of a natural mourning process which only time will heal. To ease the pain, individuals will need to externalize their feelings with the help of supportive friends, relatives or therapy. Eventually, acceptance of the loss of the marriage occurs.

For some people, there is a period of time following a divorce when they feel that a great burden has been lifted. Such individuals experience a sense of freedom and euphoria as one might have felt in adolescence.

The enthusiastically experiment in dating, sexual encounters and new social and recreational activities. There is a desperate pleasure seeking, an attempt to capture all that they felt they missed by being married. But in time these pleasures almost invariably disappoint them and they find that they need to search deeper for fulfillment.

What most divorced people come to realize is that it is necessary to work hard to rebuild a satisfying life. They learn that happiness is not a fortuitous meeting with a perfect stranger or living life in the fast lane. Instead, they must learn to integrate the lessons and experiences, good and bad, from the marriage and let go of the pain. But first, they must relearn and re-define themselves—their weaknesses as well as their strengths—their values and beliefs. In achieving this, they will experience dignity, self-esteem and autonomy. Once having established a fulfilling and happy life alone, they are prepared to invite someone else to share that life.

Constructual marital therapists have established several goals designed to help individuals through the divorce process. First, the therapist must convey to each of them that although the marriage is ending, often endings mark the beginning of something new and better. They then have to help the individuals understand that the divorce process has been in effect for a long time and a lot of the pain they are feeling is a result of that process. The therapist must help them come to the realization that there is no love, at least on the part of one of them, and this will not change. The individuals must learn to stop blaming one another and instead be helped to examine why the relationship failed and the dynamics behind the decision to divorce. During this process, the divorcing couple needs to learn to accept their own contribution to the dysfunction of the relationship. This will help to avoid the perpetuation of unresolved issues into new relationships and facilitate autonomy and differentiation.

Another important therapeutic role is to assist the individuals in examining the impact of the divorce on children, other family members, friends and other important people in their lives. Some will need help in establishing realistic expectations for child rearing so that the children can escape the shadow of the negative spiral relatively unscathed. Some will need help in achieving a fair division of property. The therapist can be effective in helping support the entire family in mourning the end of the relationship.

Finally, the therapist will need to assist the individuals in establishing new beginning and examining and planning realistic goals to maximize the potential for a successful future life for both clients.

The decision to divorce is almost never an easy one. Most couples struggle to keep the marriage together for years before deciding to separate. Divorce is an extremely painful process for everyone involved, including the therapist. There are stages of divorce through which couples must pass. If the couple can complete this process in an appropriate and healthy way, ghosts of the past will be buried. Marital therapists can play a vital role in guiding clients out of the negative spiral and toward a happier future.

To summarize this section, Constructual Marital Therapy offers the practitioner five paradigms from which to choose in meeting the specific needs of couples in conflict. Generally, following the initial interview, Marital Therapy is the method of choice to help couples resolve differences and continue their journey toward an enhancing mutual relationship. For some, the journey's goal will be the "covenant relationship." Some couples will be directed into individuation therapy in order to help resolve issues before marital therapy can progress and/or to assess whether or not Accommodation, Veritive or Divorce Therapy would be most appropriate. Accommodation Therapy is offered to those couples who are able to negotiate differences in the absence of loving feelings. If the couple is unable to achieve an accommodation relationship or make a decision to separate, Veritive Therapy is necessary. Divorce Therapy is offered to lend support and guidance to those couples who have made a decision to end their marriage.

IV

Case Presentations

INTRODUCTION

THE FOLLOWING CASES have been selected to demonstrate the practice of Constructual Marital Therapy and use the concepts presented in this work. Each example represents different and special concerns brought into therapy by the couple. In addition to demonstrating how these concerns can be best addressed, the author presents teaching methods specific to developing conceptual, planning and intervention skills.

In the first case presented, the initial interview, the therapist gathers pertinent information while assisting the couple to make immediate changes which strengthen their marriage. The following cases are classified into Constructual Marital Therapy paradigms: Marital Therapy, Individuation Therapy, Accommodation Therapy, Veritive Therapy, and Divorce Therapy. In each case the problems of the couple are examined, the degree of entrapment in the negative spiral defined, and the goals and treatment plans presented.

In defining a treatment plan, the method of treatment, i.e.: conjoint, concurrent, combined or collaborative will be disclosed. The principle of practice chosen by the therapist for the specific cases will be explained. The reader will, for example, see how such principles such as creating symmetry, building bridges, paying attention to process rather than content, and emphasizing strengths in the relationship are useful in helping couples toward a "covenant relationship."

13

THE INITIAL INTERVIEW: THE MARRIAGE OF GARY AND SALLY

EXCERPTS FROM THE CASE of Gary and Sally will illustrate how quickly the therapist can assess the dynamic of a couple, gather pertinent information which will be useful in diagnosing the marital problem, establish a treatment plan, and at the same time begin to initiate the kind of change which will allow the couple to resolve their differences. Gary, 35, is an accountant. His wife, Sally, 28, is a teacher. The couple have no children and were living separately at the time of the interview.

Gary and Sally did not begin at the enchantment phase of marriage. They clearly married for security reasons rather than feelings of recip-rocal love. They entered the marriage with minimal autonomy as both were responding to insecurities related to their respective families of origin. This resulted in their being lost in the "we psyche" as each turned to the other to be defined. Neither was ready to invite their partner to share inner feelings of self or to have their partner help toward greater self-understanding. Gary, lacking a sense of freedom in the marriage, invites Sally to control him. When Sally accepts this invitation, he passively resists as part of him wants more freedom of expression. Sally, on the other hand, is afraid she will not be accepted for herself and has chosen to try to mold Gary into her own likeness and image. When he obliges her, she becomes angry because, as she states it, "He is not his own person." At some level she recognizes that she cannot trust herself with him unless he is free to be himself. But her critical behavior keeps him distant, which serves her unconscious purpose of remaining hidden. Thus the marriage was founded on control and emotional distancing, rather than on the mutual gift of giving and enhancing. As a result, the couple's primary interactional patterns were ones of passivity versus aggressiveness.

Neither spouse entered the marriage believing him/herself to be worth loving. If they had felt lovable they would not have settled for a marriage without love. If they could not trust themselves, how could they trust their spouse to be attentive or trust that the marriage would develop into a satisfying relationship? Without mutual trust they inevitably lost hope and began to feel despair. Those feelings eventually led them to become caught in a very tight negative spiral which prevented them from passing beyond the negotiation phase of marriage and instead led to separation.

Initially, Sally and Gary were involved in collaborative therapy. Sally was seen by the author and her presenting problem was concern about her aggressive behavior and her inability to be in touch with her deeper feelings. Sally and I had a good therapeutic relationship. Shortly after treatment began, the couple decided that they wanted to try to reconcile their differences in an attempt to make the marriage work. Gary's therapist allowed me to treat the couple. The first time I met Gary was in the initial joint interview. I made a special effort to join with and support him to minimize any fear that he might have had that I was going to side with Sally. Throughout the marital therapy the couple was seen conjointly.

Following the initial joining remarks, the therapist continues the interview:

> *T:* You two have been married how long?
> *H:* Ah, it will be three years in March
> *W:* No, in May it will be two and one half years
> *H:* Sorry, you're right, it will be two and one half years
> *T:* You knew each other how long before you were married?
> *H:* (Asking wife) about a year, or two years?
> *W:* About two years.
> *T:* (to Gary) So you knew what you were getting into when you married?

H: Yeah, I've been married before, and, ah, when it happened, I think—before, I wasn't ready to get married. I think when it happened I had, ah, it was kind of, ah, she gave me a choice—either you marry me or I'm going to leave—and to me that wasn't a choice it was, ah . . . I said to myself I know what I have, and I think I have something good and I don't want to let it go. So I said fine, okay, we'll get married. I think I was ready for it. So we got married.

T: How long were you married the first time?

H: Ah, nine years, almost ten years, two months short of ten years.

T: How much time elapsed before you married Sally?

H: (Asking wife) Three years? Two years?

W: No, when I met you, you were still going through the process of divorce . . .

T: When you two married were you crazy about each other?

H: No . . . no . . . but we were comfortable with each other. I don't think I loved her, but we kind of went through with it. I think I developed a deep love for her.

T: (To wife) What was your perception of the reasons you got married?

W: My perception was that I finally found someone to marry me and that I was 26 and if I didn't get married soon, time was running out and he had a lot of good qualities I like about him, but I also realized a lot of things that were uncomfortable but I went through with the marriage anyway.

T: Gary, why did you say yes to the marriage?

H: Because I think I wanted to be with somebody, it's not like you know it was my last chance or anything like that . . . I saw her as something I needed and . . .

I noticed that Gary would turn to his wife as the authority figure even when it related to his first marriage. The current marriage appeared to be based on security reasons rather than love, although Gary later developed loving feelings for Sally. I recognized that there was not enough time for Gary to differentiate from his first wife, which reinforces his belief that Gary's subsequent marriage was at least partly based on dependency needs. I began to see that Gary and Sally have a complimentary relationship in which Sally is the dominant figure and Gary the passive or submissive partner. The interview continues, following a brief discussion about the couple's efforts to adopt a child:

T: What is your perception of why the marriage started to have problems?

H: (Who volunteers to speak first) After I can look back, from what I've read and what I've seen of myself—it was a total domination by her. I didn't have any input into it. I rarely suggested anything. I really wasn't a participant. I was more just being there and not taking the initiative to do anything. I admit I like to watch TV. I guess I was overdoing it. I'd come home every day and just watch television. She'd talk to me and not get anything out of me. I just wasn't paying any attention to her. I remember a few times when she tried to talk with me and the TV was on and she had to get right in front of me. I just wasn't paying any attention to her and that had a lot to do with it . . . she got into writing a lot of bad checks and I wouldn't even say anything. I should have told her to stop it but I figure she's taking care of it and she knows what she is doing. I felt she was in charge of it.

T: So you were more withdrawn in the relationship and she was more controlling.

H: Right.

T: Is withdrawal a pattern of yours in general?

H: I think so. It seems like it was this way in my first marriage. She was the controlling one. I didn't put a lot in it.

T: What about before then?

H: Ah, in relationships the only thing I can say is my mother controlled me a lot, and my Grandmother. I mean they had total control. If I didn't do what my mother wanted she would be angry for weeks at a time.

T: So women in your life have been dominating?

H: Yes.

T: What was your dad like?

H: He was quiet and didn't say that much. I don't remember him ever saying anything to me . . .

T: What was his relationship with your mother like?

H: He didn't have much input.

W: He was controlled.

H: My mother was a very dominating person.

T: So your perception of why problems began in your marriage was because you were withdrawn and your wife was controlling? Sally, what is your perception of why problems developed in the marriage?

W: I think what Gary said was pretty much it. I became very dominating and very, very controlling and I became the mother, the initiator. Well . . . anything I did was okay . . . there was no challenge, I was learning about growth and enhancement and different stages in the life cycle. So educationally we were going in separate directions because I felt I was really growing and I saw this man in front of the television . . . So it got to a point in my life that I said I didn't want to get up to the seventh life cycle and look back and say I wasted thirty years of my life watching this man watch television. I tried communicating with him. I tried talking with him, but we were on completely different levels. I didn't like being argumentative but I had no choice.

By this time I have concluded that the relationship is a complementary one. Gary's apparent lack of autonomy has been the result of submission, first to his mother and then to his first wife. Never having experienced freedom, Gary continues to manifest submissive behavior in his present marriage. He blames himself for the problems in his marriage and accepts full responsibility for his shortcomings. Sally criticizes herself for contribution to the problems of the marriage, but does not accept responsibility for her actions. Instead, she blames Gary. This blaming allows her to hide from her insecurities. I have developed a strategy which will be implemented indirectly. First I will attempt to change the relationship from a complementary one to a symmetrical one and I will then attempt to put Gary in charge of helping his wife. The immediate goal will be to empower Gary and thereby instill some concept of freedom and autonomy. In effect, Gary must recognize that he has the right to be understood and to have his needs met. The long term goal will be to break the pattern of one partner's being in control of the relationship so that the couple can relate in a mature way. Thus both are free to work toward a relationship of mutual respect and enhancement.

> *T:* Therefore, your differences led to a disrespect for each other?
> *H:* I think it was kind of a disrespect for myself. I didn't have any self-confidence.
> *T:* (I turn to the wife, countering the husband's pattern of taking full responsibility and trying to create some symmetry.) But you didn't like yourself either, because of the controlling person you had become.
> *W:* You're right. I don't want to be that kind of person. I would

like to be an equal partner and be able to look at my husband and think what he is saying is valid, (implying that the husband has nothing worth saying) but we were not having that.

T: (Highlighting the wife's disrespect for herself, I turn to the husband.) Did you know that she was disrespectful of herself?

H: No.

T: She was disrespectful of herself as well, so you both lost respect for yourselves.

H: (Still unable to accept an equal position with his wife.) I don't know if I ever had any at all because when I think of the past I always seem to take just what I can get. I'll take whatever I'm handed down.

T: (Countering Gary's self-disparaging remarks and working at achieving symmetry.) But did you know she had similar experiences as you in the past?

H: No.

T: (Amplifying Sally's insecurity.) Check it out with her.

W: I told you about my mother and how she tried to control me and how insecure it made me feel. I tried to balance it out by controlling you.

T: (Moving to create symmetry.) So the underlying fear you have, you just manifest it differently. Her insecurities get manifested as over–control. Your insecurities get manifested as under–control. A perfect balance for the two of you. (Amplifying the wife's weakness.) But you don't know that your wife has insecurities?

H: Not at all. The fact is that through this whole thing I had thought she was the strong one. I mean she never, ah . . . she has a cold side and that is all she showed me through the whole thing was the cold shoulder and I just, you know, through the whole thing I said I don't need that. I started building myself up and taking a look at myself and seeing where I was and found I didn't like what I saw. And so far I kind of worked on myself . . . I have a lot of feelings I was unaware of before and I can relate to them now. I know what I'm feeling now.

T: But you can see how your perceptions were distorted and she has been insecure as well.

H: Yeah, yeah.

T: It's both of you, not just one of you (turning to wife) and you recognized this as well.

W: Oh yes, I know. I know I have a lot of weaknesses and am very aware of them, but nobody points this out to me. They ignore them.

    T: (Turning to husband.) But you are going to do that from now on?

    H: Yes, I am.

The series of interventions by me helped the husband to recognize for the first time that his wife also had weaknesses. The husband is beginning to feel some power. There has been some progress toward creating symmetry. I then move on to gather more information.

    T: Why are you trying to get back together?

    W: I'm trying to make it work because I know what I have. I know I have a dependable partner. He is responsible. He will never strike me. He will always go to work. He is a good worker and there are a lot of opportunities that we can share together . . . we can travel together . . . so it's a lot for security and comfort and all the wrong things. I'm fighting getting us back together because of the intellectual differences, the communication differences. But basically I see him as a good person and I think he wasn't as bad as a lot of people. And I think I should try to hold on to that and I've seen him grow since we've split up and make some positive changes which attracted me back to him. But I've also seen these changes go down the tube, but we talked about that and I think he's aware of being sucked in by me again and now he's trying to stand up and be his own person.

    T: (To husband.) Why are you trying to get back together?

    H: I think, I mean I know that the basic things we have, love, or whatever you call it, is still there . . . no matter how shaky it is, how crumbled it was, and the comfort and everything is there. I still like to be with her but I think that since we've been apart I've missed her. Like maybe she died, I had that kind of feeling. That I really missed her and I can see all the things she can do for me. Like we can grow. . . . But the basic reason is that I love her.

Based on the couple's responses, it appears that Sally's commitment to the marriage is based on security and dependency needs and not on loving feelings. She would like Gary to change to meet her needs but not necessarily because she sees strength in him and would like to enhance that strength. Gary appears to love his wife and he believes that what she is asking of him is reasonable and in his best interest. I move on and asks each what they expect from therapy and from the therapist. They both have reasonable expectations. They hope that I will act as an impartial observer, help them to see the marital problems more clearly and help them to communicate more effectively. I then begin clinical interventions designed to lead Gary to challenge his wife and thus create more symmetry in the relationship.

I open first by creating intensity and challenging Gary by asking him if he is afraid of his wife. If Gary says no, he will be asked to prove it. During this process, I turn my body toward Gary to strengthen my ties with him and further highlight this bonding by ignoring Sally's presence.

> *T:* Before I share with you how I can help you, I need to ask you a question Gary. Are you afraid of your wife?
> *H:* Am I afraid of her?
> *T:* Yes, as a child is afraid of his mother.
> *H:* No.
> *T:* Are you sure?
> *H:* (In an assertive tone). I, no, I'm not afraid of her. I don't want to be mothered. I don't need a mother.
> *T:* But you don't have that childhood fear?
> *H:* I don't think so.
> *T:* You're absolutely sure about that?

Sally feels threatened by the intervention. She interrupts and proceeds to define how Gary is feeling:

> *W:* I don't feel Gary is afraid of me. But I think Gary sort of puts me on a pedestal and says, "Yes Sally, anything you say Sally."

I minimize her position of intrusion by simply ignoring her comments and continuing to address Gary.

> *T:* But you're sure you're not afraid of her?
> *H:* As a parental figure?
> *T:* Yes, this woman is so powerful.
> *H:* No, no. The relationship I had with my mother—I don't see anything like that—or with my father.
> *T:* But there is.
> *H:* Is there?

> *T:* Your mother was very dominant.
> *H:* Yes, the dominance was buckling under a woman.
> *T:* Sally will say she is dominant.

Sally again intrudes and begins to define Gary's feelings.

> *W:* I think he feels threatened as far as security. He thinks if I make waves for her she will walk out the door.
> *H:* Yeah.

I recognize Sally's attempts to control the interaction and perpetuate Gary's submissive behavior and move to point out and highlight Sally's behavior as inappropriate and harsh. I wish to communicate that, in effect, there is also something wrong with Sally's behavior and not just Gary's. In so doing, the theme of sameness is reinforced.

> *T:* But you have confessed that you come across hard sometimes.
> *W:* Oh yes, very hard.
> *H:* Yeah, very hard . . . like Wednesday . . . I just called her to get a little bit of reassurance and she was as cold as that wall. It was like I was talking to a wall.
> *T:* What did you say or do?
> *H:* Well, I was in the middle of letting my whole self go back to her. Everything I learned over the past three months was just gone and I was letting myself go back just totally and I didn't like it and I called her and ah, I felt rejected . . . I felt mad . . . I felt like—oh shit, what is going on? I was getting the message that she wanted to get back together and then this message said now she doesn't.
> *T:* What did you do with the anger?
> *H:* Called up a date.
> *T:* What did you do?
> *H:* I called up a date. I told myself I don't want to wait around for her. I have other things to do.

Instead of challenging his wife, Gary did what he normally does, he became passive. By calling another woman he could depend on someone to take care of him and at the same time punish his wife. I then challenged him to respond more appropriately.

T: What are you going to do next time?
H: I don't think I am going to take it so personally.

Gary again back down and takes a submissive position. I move quickly to support Gary and helps him to challenge, rather than back down from Sally.

T: Why shouldn't you take it personally?
H: Why?
T: She rejected you.
H: Yes, but everyone gets rejected.
T: Yes, but not by being treated like a wall.
H: Yeah.
T: There is a difference between being rejected and being kicked.
H: Yeah, being kicked in the teeth is what it was like.
T: Then it was a personal attack.
H: Yeah, it was a personal attack.
T: And you got angry.
H: Yeah.
T: And took out your anger by withdrawing.
H: Yeah.
T: What are you going to do next time?
H: Maybe tell her she's a bitch.

Seeing Gary's angry feelings beginning to surface, I push him to direct his feelings of anger toward his wife.

T: Try it and see what happens.

Sally interrupts to defend herself. It is expected that Gary will follow his established pattern and back down. I will need to move quickly to countermand Sally's intrusion.

W: I don't think I was being a bitch.
H: I do.
W: How I come across is cold and calculating. He calls and says all he want is a little reassurance. And he caught me at a really bad time because I'm thinking he's slipping back . . . a lot of insecurities

were coming out. Before, he was beginning to act like a person but now he was being sucked back by my influence . . .

T: She is talking to you.

H: True, and I saw it.

T: Hold it—in other words, you were coming across like a nerd?

H: When?

T: When she was rejecting you.

H: I don't think I was.

T: Well, then, she is right, you better tell her.

H: No, because all I was asking for was a little reassurance. I don't want to be told (Gary suddenly switches and begins to back down) . . . wait, maybe that is what I needed to be told because I could see myself slipping away . . .

(Sally moves in to amplify his weakness.)

W: And that bothers me, that he can't realize . . . that he needs a book to tell him.

I move quickly to counter Sally's intrusion.

T: Wait, you're changing gears on me. You said you were not coming on like a nerd and that you did not deserve the disrespect you received. Is that true or not true?

H: No, I don't deserve it.

T: You need to convince yourself. You've not done that.

H: All I wanted was a little reassurance.

W: Well I don't think I should give you any assurance . . . I do think I come across cold and calculating but I could learn a new method and say things sweeter and nicer but as of yet I don't use that method.

T: You haven't convinced her.

H: (Sigh.)

T: She's talking to you, not to me.

W: I don't want to give him any assurance.

T: Convince her you don't need to be treated like a nerd.

H: (In anger.) No! I don't need to be treated like a nerd! I'm a human being! All you had to do was say everything was fine!

Gary goes on to explain his feelings and how he wants to be treated. Sally sits quietly and listens. I will need to anchor Gary's position and do so by challenging his fear.

> *T:* Are you feeling guilty about what you are saying?
> *H:* No.

He then continues to tell Sally how he has been feeling and what he expects from the relationship. I take this opportunity to not only solidify Gary's position but to empower him.

> *T:* You know, you might have a bigger problem.
> *H:* What?
> *T:* You were saying that you were not looking to be taken care of.
> *H:* Right.
> *T:* Then she misread you. She may not be sensitive to you because that might be difficult for her and she might not know how to handle sensitivity. She knows how to handle dependency. But when you come across wanting normal support, she might not recognize it and that could be a big problem for you.

Gary, feeling free to be himself, turns to his wife and shares in detail how insensitive she has been in regard to his feelings and that she perceives the expression of loving feelings as a weakness. Sally does not become defensive, but listens. I bring closure to the scenario by putting Gary in charge of Sally.

> *T:* You are going to have to help her to understand soft feelings.
> That is her problem and she recognizes that.
> *H:* How do I do that?
> *T:* By talking and sharing your feelings.

I have been successful in first creating symmetry in the session and then putting Gary in the position of helping Sally. The session continues with me teaching the couple what is required of an enhancing relationship and how he can and cannot help. They are given a homework assignment and asked to return the following week. For the next few weeks Gary becomes increasingly aggressive but eventually he become assertive. The couple develops a symmetrical relationship and by the end of therapy they have resolved their major differences. They move back in together and proceed with plans to adopt a child.

In addition to the information gathering process, the emphasis in this session was to change the passive–aggressive interactional pattern this couple exhibited. In so doing, the couple learned to communicate as mature adults. This allowed them to ultimately resolve differences which had created emotional distance for years. This process also facilitated individual growth and development as it led both partners toward a path of greater autonomy.

I used primarily supportive interventions to empower Gary. I maintained balance by always respecting the dignity of both partners, by asking both spouses the same basic questions and by asking Sally to comment on her own insecurities. The latter was crucial for the criticism was then not coming from me, but instead reflected Sally's own true feelings about herself. I did not focus on content, but instead built upon the process which maintained the complimentary aspect of the relationship. I helped Sally and Gary build a bridge of feelings between each other. This strengthened Gary's position in the relationship, something they both needed. The process helped Sally to address her feelings, something she had requested assistance with. I was able to translate Gary's feelings into actions by helping him to convey his angry feelings directly to Sally. It was evident in this session that the couple saw me as an expert. It was also clear from the tape of this session that I was in control of directing the interview.

14

MARITAL THERAPY: THE MARRIAGE OF GREG AND JEAN

THE CASE OF GREG AND JEAN demonstrates how a marriage cannot only withstand a major catastrophe but be strengthened by it if the couple has established a strong foundation for the relationship. This case also illustrates how effective therapy can be when the therapist begins with and stays focused on the results of a crisis rather than the reasons the crisis occurred. Finally this case demonstrates how conflict can heal rather than destroy a relationship.

Greg is a thirty–two year old electrical engineer. His first marriage had lasted for approximately two years and ended when his wife, Trish, died giving birth to their son, Joshua. A year after the tragedy he met and subsequently fell in love with Jean. A year after meeting they were married. Jean is a thirty-one year old homemaker. On entering therapy, they had been married eight years and had two mutual children, Susie, five, and Tommy, two. The couple had achieved a covenant relationship in which there was profound trust, attentiveness and enjoyment of each other's company. Each perceived the other as a loving parent to the children.

The couple's problems began two years previously when they agreed to have a second child. Jean was very enthusiastic about another child, but Greg was hesitant. His reluctance was associated with the major difficulty that Jean had in pregnancy and childbirth with their first born and great fear associated with his memory of Trish's death in childbirth. He was also apprehensive about the additional financial and emotional responsibility of raising a third child. Although he suggested to Jean that he did have concerns about having another child, he did not fully declare to her, or to himself the depth of his ambivalence. Part of the reason he did not express himself was that Jean was so enthusiastic about the idea that he did not want to disappoint her.

Greg's fear was realized when Jean did indeed have difficulty with her pregnancy. Although Greg felt strong, loving feelings toward Tommy, he began to feel burdened with the added responsibility. He believed that he could not express these thoughts to Jean as it would only create pain for her. But he became burdened with the feelings and began to withdraw and feel a deep depression. At the anniversary of Trish's death he became more depressed. Greg had always felt depression at the anniversary of the tragedy. Greg fell into the natural trap of not wanting to burden or create pain for Jean and for himself and so he did not reveal himself to her.

Greg finally shared his burden with Carole, a colleague to whom he was attracted. The sharing of his problems led to a brief affair, which only added guilt to the burden he was carrying. Jean was perceptive enough to see that something had changed and she was able to get Greg to tell her the truth about the liaison. This resulted in a major crisis in the marriage. A fundamental contract had been broken, that of exclusiveness. Although he did not intend to hurt Jean, he did in fact betray her. As will be seen in the following excerpts from an interview, Jean became infuriated and expressed righteous anger, an anger based on having one's dignity attacked as opposed to an anger based on insecurity. As with all crises, shock, disbelief, anger, confusion and helplessness set in and was experienced by both Greg and Jean.

For nine months the couple had not been able to recover from the crisis. Although daily conflicts arose, the couple never did get caught in the negative spiral. They attacked issues, not each other's dignity. They never lost sight of their love for one another and made efforts to be sympathetic and understanding with each other. They wanted to rebuild their marriage, but they didn't have the tools. They finally sought the assistance of a therapist and were referred to me.

The first question I asked the couple was, "What happened?" I did not ask why it happened. They would, of course, indicate some of the "whys," but I wanted to emphasize what actually resulted from the devastating event and in so doing I focused upon the actual rather than the speculative. If the traditional approach of concurrent therapy was applied, endless hours would be spent trying to determine why it happened, the implied insecurities which led to the event and how the couple could problem solve the issue. In so doing, I would not allow the most powerful forces to influence the resolution of the crisis. The most important of these forces is the concern the spouses have for each other. This concern leads to a freeing of the healing power of the loving relationship. Finally, the freedom both have to be themselves and thus be free to help one another to heal the relationship.

In deciding to work with this couple conjointly, I could make use of the natural forces and provide a positive atmosphere and conceptual framework within which the couple could use the crisis to add greater depth to their relationship rather than let the crisis become a divisive factor. Initially, I built a number of bridges in the marriage. In particular, I emphasized the loving feelings both continued to experience toward each other. I then made clear to the couple that their response to the crisis was perfectly normal and expected. In so doing, both were validated for being themselves. How could Jean not feel betrayed and lose profound trust when for seven years she had had complete faith in her husband's fidelity. Her expression of anger, confusion and lack of trust were predictable feelings when she learned of the affair. Greg would predictably feel guilty as well as defenseless and overwhelmed by Jean's feelings.

It was natural for both to feel helpless and doubtful about the future of their relationship. They fell into the natural trap of trying to avoid painful encounters rather than deal with them and thus allowing the emotional wounds to heal. The couple was instructed to find time daily to share the pain and not try to problem solve. They were to simply share their feelings and beliefs. This task would allow for a structure in which the couple would feel more control over their problems and thus begin to problem solve the issue. Further, in a loving relationship, spouses do not wish to see their partner in pain, no matter how hurt they themselves feel. We will see this in the following interview. They give each other the gift of being attentive to each other's needs. They are there for on another. Since the healing process takes a long time, the couple is seen every other week and then every three weeks. The following interview is the third in a six week period. To assist the couple in learning to handle the helplessness experienced when in conflict, I discuss with them the way they handle anger and then encourage angry feelings to be expressed in the session. Immediately following Jean's description of an issue that made her angry, I turned to Greg and asked how he responded to her feelings:

    H: Well, we tried to talk about it and that . . . ah, that didn't . . . that wasn't really what she was looking for. I guess I don't know. I, ah, I just kind of listen a lot, I think.
    T: And how do you feel afterward?
    H: I don't know . . . I don't feel angry at her or anything like that. It's part of what I caused by what I did and it's something I have to sort of help her through. (Greg takes responsibility for his behavior.)
    T: How did you feel afterward?
    W: Basically I had a hard time believing anything he says because I feel like it's subject to change. He has pointed out in his behavior that we . . . in my opinion were having a good relationship. I had no idea that there was something wrong and so I just don't believe him when he says things like that. I believe that he is just saying it. Just to shut me up . . . or make me feel better. Not because he really means it you know. His response is—"You know how I feel." I feel very distrustful and that makes me mad because it's not supposed to be that way. (This is a normal response given that she had absolute trust for seven years.)
    T: The anger comes with the frustration because right now there seems to be no end to it.
    W: Yeah. (After a long phase I ask Jean to describe further what made her angry.)
    W: We were having a nice dinner and I . . . when he talks about people I get . . . there was this woman in the restaurant. He kept mentioning her. I asked "Did you know her?" because he kept watching her and he knew she wasn't eating her pie or whatever . . . and I said why are you watching her eat her dinner, or why, period, are you paying so much attention to her . . . to someone you don't even know. I got really upset with that. Number one . . . he would come home and talk with me about other women in the office. I thought this is really nice. I'm glad these people are being nice to him, Carole would bring him hamburgers, talk to him, be hospitable

to him make him feel good—you know be a really nice person to
him. And he could come home and tell me what a nice person she was
to him. And now whenever he mentions anything like that I get very,
very upset. I really thought he knew her (the woman in the restaurant)
. . . and sometimes I think he knows everybody. (Her pain begins to
surface and she becomes tearful.) I know it's crazy, I know it's not true.
And that's just part of it . . . but I feel like . . . my God, do you have
, . . I get very angry because I feel he's turned into one of them. I
believe he has someone else in his office . . . before I always felt good.
My husband doesn't do that . . . he would come home and tell me
what those jerks would do . . . it really upsets me.

T: What have you been experiencing, Greg?

H: Like what happened at dinner. I understand what she is
saying but I, you know . . . (he describes the celebration in which the
woman at the restaurant was a participant.) . . . I mentioned to Jean
what was happening.

That touches off a painful cord in Jean.

W: Well, you have to admit she took a real good look at you.

H: Well I wasn't looking at her.

W: (Jean now expresses her anger while crying.) Well, that's
tough, but she took a real good look at you.

H: That's not my fault.

W: It was like you knew her.

H: I don't know her . . . I can understand why you could be
angry at me but I don't know her.

W: It's not unfair for me to think this.

H: You're right, it's not unfair for you to think that.

W: Well, I think that I'm going to think that no matter how
much I tell myself well, that's not true . . . you're (meaning herself)
crazy (crying profusely) and I'm acting like an idiot . . . and I can't
stop.

T: Or you don't want to.

W: Or I don't want to. How do you stop? How do you imagine
he is not with every woman in town? How do you make yourself an
adequate person in his eyes? He says that you are, but then . . . oh,
how can you be if this happened? How could you be that person you
thought you were if this happened? There must be something wrong
with me if this happened. I feel this.

H: I told you that I don't think there was anything wrong with you.

W: . . . but it doesn't seem like that's the kind of way it is. I think he blamed me for the baby without telling me, and therefore he acted out and did this . . . 'cause he didn't tell me but we still had the baby.

H: I should have told you.

W: (Screaming) That's not fair!

H: I know it's not fair!

W: (Expressing deep pain.) Why punish me for something you didn't tell me? Why punish me?

The session continues with a long discussion of the events and discussions that led to having the baby and the incident of Greg's affair. Greg shares his view but is not defensive. However, Jean believes he is trying to justify his actions and she speaks to that question. Believing that the couple has shared enough on the issues, I attempt to bring the session back to a positive note by asking if there was anything positive about their recent trip.

W: Yes, after I had my moment of anger, the rest of the time went very nicely.

The remainder of the session focuses on the positive things in the relationship. The above excerpts indicate the appropriate confusion, anger and mistrust Jean feels because of Greg's infidelity. She does not attack him but shares her despair. Without her being aware of the reasons, Jean is feeling safe to express herself. Jean is able to express these strong feelings partly because of her own inner strength and partly because Greg is allowing himself to be there, listen and validate her pain. Greg never becomes defensive and on several occasions validates Jean's right to feel and believe in the way she does. Equally important, he does not patronize her. He only does what he can to support her. Greg feels free to behave openly because he has achieved autonomy and because he knows that Jean is expressing feelings that come out of deep feelings of love for him. His freedom is expressed in his taking respon-sibility for what he did but also to challenge what he believes to be unfair accusation. He does not stop her from speaking her truth but he does correct what he believes are incorrect perceptions. Although they do not fully understand it, this conflictual but supportive, albeit very painful process, will allow healing to take place. Jean believes by understanding what happened she will be relieved of her pain. This process of externalizing painful feelings and accepting responsibility will eventually heal the marriage. This process will add greater depth to their friendship as in sharing the pain they are experiencing at the deepest level as well as the gift of giving and receiving love. Inroads of change can be seen by the seventh session. Arguments still persist, but they are less frequent and less intense. Throughout this session the partners are in one way or another, holding each other.

T: How have you two been?

H: We've had some moments but we've been able to talk things through much better. What do you think? (To Jean.)

W: We went to San Francisco a few weeks ago. We had a wonderful time but then later I began to think maybe he didn't have a good time. I was beginning to get very upset. That was what he was saying wasn't true. I could tell on a day to day basis that he seemed to be enjoying himself and that he seemed to be enjoying my company, but then I got very upset on the last day. I told him that I . . . that if I really believed that he was having a good time . . . perhaps he was doing this . . . I don't know. Then I got really upset because we were having a good time and I didn't (tearful) want to come home.

H: We had a really good time.

(They went on to describe their vacation which Greg continues to maintain was a good one.)

H: I don't blame her for doubting me, but sincerely I really had a wonderful time. We had a great time . . . we already planned our next time together.

T: What did you take away from our last session?

H: That we needed to continue talking even after we hit the argument stage which is a point where a lot of times we have our positions and we want to defend those positions. And I think this time, while we have had a couple of arguments since then, naturally, and recently (he goes on to describe the latest conflict) . . . we got into a real argument then because I . . . I sometimes get the feeling you're not really looking forward to my coming home. And in some ways I feel that's true because when I'm home, then we have to deal with it and when I'm away, even though she misses me terribly and I miss her terribly, there's not the potential for conflict . . .

W: I tried to explain. It's not so much not wanting you to be there because I miss you terribly. You don't believe that.

H: But I do.

The couple later discuss Greg's being away at a retreat.

W: When you were gone, it drove me nuts. It drove me crazy because there was nothing I could do. I didn't have control over what you were doing. I would have to leave it up to you and I felt like it had been left up to you before and it always came down to that and I don't like that. It always comes down to that . . . I have such a hard time with it (she describes her difficulty further) . . . I feel like I have to get to re-know him. Like I have to find out what he is like all over again and that is sometimes uncomfortable because I had this . . . I had this idea of what he was before and now that's not there anymore.

T: What do you think about what she said?

H: I think it will take a long time. I don't see how she can get away from that kind of feeling because it is the focal point of everything. And ah, after we continued to talk that night she didn't want to talk to me and there was a lot of hostility and everything and I was trying to talk and I'm not trying to paint myself as the good guy because at one point in the evening I was going to say "the hell with it"'cause I was getting kind of worn down. But we kept on talking and then finally sort of broke the barrier and ended the evening well. Do you think . . . and we sat and talked for a long time and it really ah, hurts, me a lot when she . . . when she's hurting that much . . . and I don't like it and I get angry then. I get very angry with myself because I know I'm the cause of that . . . of that anger or sorrow or sadness and everything else she feels toward me. And I get so upset over that . . . I get really angry but we sat down and spent a little time crying together and . . . but I get really, ah frustrated because I know those are the feelings she is going to have and there is nothing I can do during those moments to stop the pain she is in . . . and it's a hard time, but I think that particular evening . . . it wasn't the most fun evening we ever had but I think it ended with us feeling better.

W: Sometimes it's strange after you go through that you feel better.

H: You kind of got it out of your system and went through it together.

W: Well that's more of it than anything because later on, toward evening instead of . . . instead of getting defensive and instead of blaming yourself instead of getting angry with yourself there came a point in the discussion in the talk, where you started to tell me how you felt you were feeling and how you . . . you hurt too. And some-times . . . sometimes you don't do that. Lately you've been doing it because Marshall has explained it and you know that's what I need to hear you say. And it sounds funny but I don't want to hear you berate yourself—I just want to hear you say how terrible you feel.

Even though Jean is still in pain, she is still attentive to Greg's pain. (It is in that way that they bond.)

W: It doesn't make me feel better . . . but it makes me feel like I'm not alone and that's important because I do worry when you're gone . . . and then Friday . . .

I intervene before she moves on to a content area. I need to high-light and anchor the feelings experienced and the changes made. I also wish to have the couple leave with a framework of understanding which will continue the growth being experienced.

T: Before you go I would like to make some comments. I think it is really crucial in regard to what is happening. Often couples see conflict as being divisive and as a reflection of not caring. That is sometimes true, but in your case the conflict represents just the opposite and that needs to be recognized. The pain is coming from all the love you feel for each other. When you argue or get upset or if you are sharing pain it is a reflection of love, no inattentiveness. You must not lose sight of what is happening. It is a reflection of your closeness that you feel each other's pain. Secondly, as you have indi-cated, Greg, you can't fix it for Jean. It's true. You can't take her pain away but when you engage her the way you do you help to heal her pain. And healing takes time. You can't fix it, but you can help it to heal. So when you share her pain, and hear her pain, she is healing inside. And the only way to heal is to continue to participate in this kind of exchange. That's absolutely necessary.

Three, and this is crucial—you said, Jean, that he is part of you when you go through this process together, that you feel better. But that's true because you are sharing in your pain and most of us think that we need to share loving feelings, and we do, but we add greater depth to love when we can share our pain and very few people can do that. When you share each other's pain you are making loving sacrifices. Are you not? You are—because you don't have to be there. Because you participate. Listen, you are giving of yourself even though it is painful to do so. So if you are giving a loving sacrifice, at a very deep level, reciprocally, that's where the feeling of closeness originates.

W: It seems hard to believe.

T: But that is what happens.

W: Yes, that is what happens.

T: (Pushing for a deeper internalization of what has been said.) So it is three things. The conflict represents love and in that process you are healing and in healing you are making loving sacrifices which is experienced as being together.

W: I see what you mean . . . I see what you mean because even though at that particular point you're not feeling loving toward your partner you are still giving that person love because of the conflict and the sharing of pain and that's where it comes from.

T: And people assume that love always feels good.

W: It seems to make me feel better in a way that . . . after an argument and we get to the level where we can just be two people not fighting . . . like I said before when it gets down to what is really there . . . it seems to make me feel better that he has told me that he hurts too. Yeah, it make sense.

I continue to amplify on the concepts that I have articulated. Toward the end of the session Greg talks about the need to continue discussing issues.

H: I still have a reluctance to talk because of what she goes through. It was really ridiculous the other night, I thought. We were going through this and I started feeling kind of down and the next thing I know I'm crying and then she starts taking care of me. I told her this is not the way its supposed to be. But now I guess it really is, but it feels unfair to her . . . but I guess if she didn't love me she wouldn't be able to do that, I guess.

T: It is a gift. It has nothing to do with fairness, it has to do with love.

H: Yeah.

I then close the session by reiterating the three points that I want the couple to remember. Throughout the treatment I primarily used supportive and cognitive interventions. This engaged the spouses in an interactional pattern which brought them closer together by pointing out how the conflict they experienced represented love rather than a lack of attention to one another. In so doing, the love they have for each other allowed them to heal themselves. Greg and Jean brought into the marriage their own maturity, positive self-esteem and intact dignity. They wished to share a life of love and happiness when they married. Throughout their marriage they invited each other to share in their inner selves and sought to know and understand each other. This manner of interacting continued throughout their time of crisis and was eventually the medium with which they healed their wounds.

When a crisis such as an affair occurs after a couple has established an enhancing relationship, the loving energy that has accumulated is not depleted. This energy has been created by the sharing of friendship, the bond of trust and the giving of loving sacrifices. With the proper support, the couple can call upon this energy reserve to fuel the loving feelings of the relationship. The case of Greg and Jean clearly illustrates this point. Although both were devastated by Greg's affair, they called upon the credibility that had been established in the marriage to overcome this crisis and strengthen the relationship. The same "straw that can break a camel's back" can be the "tie that binds" a couple together in an even more loving marriage.

15

MARITAL THERAPY: THE MARRIAGE OF FRANK AND CINDY

THE CASE OF FRANK AND CINDY illustrates the constructive use of a trial separation combined with marital therapy. Frank is twenty-seven years old and he is working toward a paramedic license. Cindy is twenty-six and a part-time waitress. They have been married for five years and have a four year old son. Frank has an extensive social network while Cindy's chief source of emotional support is her mother. Cindy's parents live two blocks away and are in daily contact with her. About six months into the dating relationship Cindy had begun to have doubts about her feelings for Frank, although she never doubted his love for her. Conflict arose during that time but Cindy discovered that she was pregnant and she married Frank out of a feeling of obligation. She was also pressured into the marriage by her mother. The couple did not enjoy the enchantment phase of marriage as conflicts became more severe immediately following the marriage. Another factor in the disharmony was the fact that the couple did not have time to adjust to the marriage after the birth of their son, Jason. The parenting responsibilities added additional stress and areas of conflict to the marriage.

When seen in therapy, the couple was severely enmeshed in the negative spiral. Little autonomy was exhibited and each continuously attacked the dignity of the other. There was daily bickering. Cindy believed Frank to be insensitive to her. She felt he was critical, neglectful and not supportive of her needs or desires. Frank believed that there was nothing he could do to please his wife. When he tried to involve her with his friends she did not participate. When he bought her gifts they were not pleasing to her. When he tried to repair things, she felt they were not done correctly. To cope with the constant fighting, Frank began associating more with his friends. To meet her needs Cindy became involved with another man.

The couple entered therapy when Frank discovered that Cindy was having an affair. Cindy had agreed to end the extra-marital relationship. Instead of separating, the couple agreed to try marital counseling.

Initially, the couple was seen in conjoint marital sessions. I was able to assist the couple in effective communication and in problem solving issues that had impacted the marriage for years. The couple spent more time together and began to participate in joint activities. But they were both unhappy with the relationship. Finally, I separated them and asked each if they had ambivalent feelings about continuing the marriage. Frank said that he did not. Cindy stated that she had seen her lover again and was extremely ambivalent about staying married to Frank. She said that she had felt trapped into the marriage because she was pregnant with Jason and furthermore her mother has pressured her into the marriage. She was envious of Frank because he was able to pursue a career while she felt stuck in a primary caretaking position.

A therapist can often assist a couple in dealing with issues which have to do with the past and with feelings of ambivalence. In therapy, a couple can learn to recognize and nurture positive feelings that exist in the present stage of the relationship. If successful, this mutual sharing of love will over-ride the pain of the past and these pains will slowly heal and then disappear. Efforts to accomplish these goals failed in this case example. Although the couple was able to communicate effectively, they did not feel a reciprocal closeness. I decided that Cindy' ambivalence had to be directly addressed and encouraged the couple to proceed with a planned trial separation. Both partners understood that Cindy must feel free to be in the marriage and that the purpose of the separation had advantages and disadvantages. I told the couple that in his experience the large majority of couples who separate go on to divorce. They experience and overcome the pain, fear and insecurities associated with a divorce. Dependency needs are overcome. With adequate autonomy established there can be a clear recognition that love does not exist. This allows the spouses to initiate a divorce. In some cases however, when the dependency and fears are resolved, there is an awareness that love does still exist and the couple will continue the marriage.

In this case the separation was very structured. The couple returned their wedding rings to each other to symbolize that they were no longer emotionally married. Frank remained in the home while Cindy returned to her mother with Jason. The couple planned the caretaking of the household responsibilities. Frank was put in charge of the bills. They could see and date each other but not in their own home. This was to reinforce the idea that they were no longer married. They arranged custody visits for Jason as if they were divorced. They agreed on how they would tell their family and friends about the separation.

The separation was set for three months at which time the couple could extend the agreement. Having a fixed date in mind often facilitates the intensity which leads to clear decision making. Couples feel the pressure in having to work to accomplish their goals. The three month period was decided on because it had been my experience that it takes about that amount of time to resolve feelings of ambivalence.

The couple agreed that they had the freedom to date with no questions asked. Frank recognized that Cindy needed complete freedom in order for her to make a clear decision. By his supporting her request, Cindy recognized how much Frank loved her and wanted to be in the relationship. A bridge was established. By allowing Cindy to date, Frank alleviated the problems and mystery of her having an affair. If one or both wanted a divorce, divorce therapy would be offered. If they agreed that they wanted to continue the marriage they would renew their vows, return the rings and participate in marital therapy.

The renewing of vows create an event which gives public notice that the couple is back together and makes a statement to one another about their desire to maintain a loving relationship. It also assists in the internalization that a decision has been made.

During the separation, I saw the couple in concurrent individuation therapy. They would work on the feelings, issues and behaviors associated with the separation. Seeing them concurrently reinforced the idea that they were separate and each had to make a separate decision regarding whether or not to continue the relationship. Often it is the person who was not initially ambivalent about the marriage who makes the decision to leave. This is partially due to the fact that the non-ambivalent partner was denying the conflict in the marriage and deny his/her lack of loving feelings. A trial separation will often serve to break down that denial.

In structuring a separation according to the above guidelines, I exercised the principle of practice to create a process (here again the emphasis on process) which allows couples to address their problems in a real way. In this case, he was able to recreate the engagement period. It was also important that Cindy addressed the issue of feeling forced into the marriage and her feeling of envy that Frank was successful in his work. Cindy once again had the choice of deciding whether or not to be married to Frank.

When Cindy returned home, the conflict with her mother was rekindled. Her mother immediately insisted that Cindy return to Frank. But Cindy was no longer financially dependent on Frank as she now saw possible career opportunities for herself.

Cindy's lover was invited to participate in therapy with her. This was to assist me in better assessing the nature of the extra–marital relationship and to demystify and de–romanticize the involvement. Cindy saw that the affair did not represent a loving relationship but was a means by which she could have some of her needs met and feel supported. The relationship with her lover ended. Some therapists would not ask the lover of a client to attend treatment as this could be interpreted as a betrayal by the other spouse. But I believe it is possible to remain neutral in such a situation and the information gathered might be vital for the treatment of the marriage.

After assisting Cindy in recognizing her dependency needs, her mother was invited to attend a session but the mother refused to attend. I was able to work using family of origin concepts and interventions to assist Cindy in establishing an adult relationship with her mother. She felt free to make her own decisions and she no longer believed that her mother controlled her life. I was then able to assist Cindy in considering career opportunities.

During the course of the treatment Frank and Cindy began dating. At the end of a three month period, Cindy's love for Frank had been rekindled. They renewed their vows and continued in conjoint marital therapy.

Separations need to be well structured with clearly defined goals. If this is not true they worsen the relationship and prevent spouses from addressing important issues. In this case, the emphasis was on autonomy and the importance to Cindy of being free in the marriage. To accomplish this task, a process had to be created where she had a choice. In addition, the individuation issues associated with her mother needed to be addressed. Finally, to help her with the issue of her envy of Frank's business accomplishments she needed to develop a plan for her own career.

Several therapeutic models were applied in treating this couple. These included marital therapy, family of origin work, strategic therapy and behavioral therapy. In this case significant other people were asked to participate in treatment. Finally, although it was Cindy who was ambivalent about the marriage, I did not lose sight of the important issues that Frank was dealing with and his need for support.

16

INDIVIDUATION THERAPY: THE MARRIAGE OF JAMES AND OLGA

THE CASE OF JAMES AND OLGA illustrates the effective use of a family of origin approach in individuation therapy. James is a thirty-three year old teacher who, at the time he entered therapy, was unemployed because he refused to work. His wife, Olga, is a thirty-two year old nurse. The couple had been married for nine years and appeared to be in the integration stage of marriage. Until one year prior to therapy, the couple had shared an extensive social network, seldom argued and experienced love for one another.

Approximately a year previously, Olga began expressing a desire to start a family. James did not want a child and they began arguing over that issue. The arguments spread to other areas of the marriage. James began to feel more and more dissatisfied with everything. The couple came to therapy because they did not want the marriage to deteriorate. They were intuitive enough to seek help before a negative spiral began. The initial presenting problem was wanting help in deciding whether or not to have a baby. In the initial session it was evident that James was severely despondent and had in fact quit teaching out of his despair over the institution's ability to teach in what he felt was a chaotic world. Olga was unaware of James' suicidal ideation. She knew he was depressed because he always felt tired, he no longer wished to be with friends and he stopped being sexually active, but she did not realize the extent of his depression.

In the initial session James described his parents as cruel, uncaring, rigid and alcoholic. When he first described his childhood he assumed a fetal position and cried hysterically. He sobbed "Who would want to bring a child into this sick world!" It was clear that James's world view was associated with unresolved family of origin issues. I was able to have James work on his depression before making a decision about fathering a child. I believed James's negative feelings about having a baby were influenced by his depression. James refused to have Olga in the sessions and so the spouses were seen in concurrent therapy. Before the session ended, James was referred to a psychiatrist for anti-depression medication.

While some therapists do not believe that it is ever important to address family of origin issues, I believe that a problem which might have begun thirty years ago remains a problem until it is resolved. If a client feared his father when he was twelve, it is a current problem if that fear is still causing conflict now that the client is thirty. It is my belief that all family problems are current issues which may or may not be associated with unresolved past conflicts. This belief allows me to accept many of the theoretical concepts developed by Bowen, Boszormenyi-Nagy, Framo, Haley, and Minuchin for explicating family development and function while utilizing principles of practice supported by Haley and Minuchin for planning and intervention in treatment.

On the surface, the attempt to help clients define an adult relationship with their parents after childhood fears and angers have dominated most of their lives seems a formidable task. It is possible, if approached correctly, for a client to engage and to be able to resolve family of origin conflicts. I help the client to come to the realization that it is possible to take control, establish reasonable expectations and have a realistic relationship with these figures who are real people beyond the role of the client's parents. Often it is a matter of helping the client put in the past the insecurities, feelings of helplessness and constant fight to win the love of the parent. Issues of control are discussed, the feelings of dependent child and the reality that adult strength and confidence be used to integrate the past into a new reality in which one can redefine experiences as a mature adult.

Clients often have unrealistic expectations of their parents' ability to love, nurture, or to even behave in a socially acceptable way. It is a fact of love that filial feelings of loyalty transcend even the worst parenting and it is on this loyalty that I depend when helping clients work on family of origin problems. I must, however, assist the clients in recognizing that they cannot force their parents to make any changes, including developing an ability to show love. But with the knowledge that the parent would have wanted to love them, would have wanted to provide a secure home, would not have consciously hurt them, but did not themselves have all power or wisdom or strength—the client comes to control his/her own relationship with the parent and it becomes possible to integrate negative experiences in a positive way.

Even the worst childhoods had some moments of joy. The client tends to see the past as negative and his/her parents only as critical parents with no appreciation for anything good that might have happened. This concept coincides with object–relations theory, which states that children incorporate highlights of reality, either positive or negative, and carry them into their present narrow, often distorted view, of what happened. I can help clients broaden their view of reality, correct distortions of the past and understand their parents in their many roles. This can be accomplished by helping clients recognize that many of their positive attributes and strengths come from their early relationship with their parents. It helps the client to learn that there were many factors which were important in their childhood experience:

1. Parents feel responsibility for the growth and development of their children and this becomes manifested in a desire for perfect behavior from the child.

2. Parents invest much of themselves in their children.

3. Child-rearing practices are primarily learned from one's own childhood experiences.

4. Parents have a life apart from child–rearing, including having to deal with their own marital relationship.

By encouraging clients to work with their parents, it often becomes evident that the parents wish to establish a positive relationship. It is an unfortunate reality that many couples have children before they are mature enough to raise a family. Parents of adult children, now mature themselves, often regret some of their past behaviors and are anxious to start a new relationship on an adult–adult level, but will rarely initiate the resolution of conflicts. It is difficult to admit ignorance or incompetence, especially in so important a role.

Therapists can help clients recognize that parents do the best they can and some of the things that happened were unavoidable. Clients often blame their parents for the clients' own weaknesses and behaviors and thus avoid taking responsibility for negative actions and feelings. Blaming also gives them a feeling of control—an explanation for their own inexplicable behavior. This behavior is often later displaced onto the spouse as a device to deal with a dysfunctional marriage. In this case, rather than talk about his problems or work them through with transference, James was encouraged to visit his parents even though they lived in another state. He reluctantly agreed and began by writing a letter as this was his least threatening course of action. He was later able to phone and finally to visit. In so doing, James was able to correct distorted perception and to recognize that his role in his family of origin was that of scapegoat. In so doing, he took charge of his feelings, asserted and created autonomy for himself as he began to control his participation in the relationship. He also felt that his dignity had been restored. James's parents actually changed very little but he was now able to accept their imperfections. Throughout this experience, James was able to transfer his new insights and assertiveness into other areas of his life. He returned to work and he and Olga participated in marital therapy and were able to re–establish a happy marriage. Following treatment, the couple decided to have a child. It is often the case, however, that when individuals complete family of origin work they cannot resolve differences in the marriage and will divorce.

17

INDIVIDUATION THERAPY: THE MARRIAGE OF GARY AND NANCY

A COMMON PROBLEM that couples bring to therapy is ambivalence about staying in the marriage. Generally, if the ambivalence is mild, I will provide marital therapy on the assumption that if the relationship is strengthened, the couple will decide to remain together. If, however, the ambivalence is profound, efforts to establish a satisfactory marriage will fail due to a lack of commitment from one or both partners. This issue will need to be directly addressed in individuation therapy.

Gary, 33, is a corporate supervisor who began therapy when he became despondent over the possibility of an impending divorce. He and his wife, Nancy, were then separated. Nancy, 29, had completed a BS degree and was a homemaker. They met and married while in college. When they married, Nancy was sure of her love for Gary. Gary had private reservations about Nancy. They have been married nine years and have three children: Kenny, 6, Katie, 3, and Judy, 2.

It was evident in the first session with Gary that he was feeling extremely depressed and overwhelmed with issues associated with a possible divorce. He listed his major concerns: a reluctance to hurt Nancy, a fear of failure, a fear of what his friends and business associates would think, and a desire to maintain an intact home for his three children. As this would be the first divorce in the extended family, he was also concerned about what his family would feel.

The second session, with Nancy in attendance, allowed me to recognize that Gary and Nancy had a complementary relationship. Gary is quiet and passive in the relationship and Nancy is assertive and direct. On the surface, it appeared as if the couple had reached the integration phase of marriage, but they were actually stuck in the negotiation stage. Conflicts arose over many issues in the marriage but were never directly addressed or resolved. Instead, Gary kept his feelings and needs to himself which propelled Nancy to act decisively. As time passed, Gary's repressed anger turned into resentment which led to profound distrust and emotional distancing. Nancy was not aware of Gary's deep feelings of distrust until he asked for a separation. She was to later learn that Gary's resentment about the marriage was present before the birth of the last two children.

Nancy realized that she could do nothing to influence Gary's decision about leaving the marriage. Initially, she agreed to wait until he resolved the issue in therapy. She attended the sessions until she went on an extended vacation.

In the second session, I engaged Gary in individuation therapy, using an approach found effective in breaking obsessive thought patterns. Gary obsesses on the thought that by leaving the marriage, he might be making the wrong decision. In the first session, I move to reduce his obsessiveness by suggesting that he forget about making a decision and instead concentrate on the issues which keep him indecisive. He will then vacillate from one issue to another. I believe his fears regarding these issues are really the same, whether the issue is countermanding a family value or hurting his children. By moving him to his primary feelings about why he fears divorcing Nancy, I hope to free him from his fears so that he might actively respond to each issue presented.

Excerpts from the second session will illustrate how I prepare Gary to examine his feelings. This session also demonstrates the intervention techniques used and the difficulty of helping a client move to and remain in primary feelings. Following introductory remarks to the clients and informing Nancy of treatment goals formulated in the first session, I begin working with Gary.

> *H:* I think the big one for me is to identify the fears and concerns I have . . . ah. . . about making a decision and understanding ah . . . trying to get in touch with what I feel . . . somehow.
> *T:* What stood out in my mind last week was that you had six

or seven major areas of concern. You articulated these very well. You finally passed the "shoulds." You were able to identify what those concerns were—missing your kids, wanting to influence their behavior, not wanting to feel responsible for hurting your wife, that fear of hurting your parents . . . there are seven variables and if you don't isolate them it's like one massive feeling of being stuck. If we can compartmentalize them and take them one at a time we should be able to get in touch with feelings associated with each issue. And if we do that more and more, what you truly feel will unfold before you.

You had one major stumbling block in your head and that is "Am I going to make the right decision?" and I said to you, "If you stay with that question, you are going to remain stuck. That's down the road. You won't know if you made the right decision. But if you drop that question and, instead, get in touch with each of these issues and if you begin to make things happen, and you begin being you, rather than what you should be, the outcome will provide a decision that will feel right no matter what happens. Perhaps not completely right, because with major issues there is usually some doubt, but almost completely right." In other words, you need to concentrate on the process rather than on the decision itself. Have you been able to block thinking about whether or not this is the right decision?

H: No, I haven't. And . . . ah . . . I guess that's . . . ah . . . I don't know. There's a lot of times when I feel there's no time to do the things I got to do. There's a lot of pressure there . . . ah . . . commitments, to my family . . . to my parents . . . to my work. I don't seem to have enough time alone. When I do have time alone ah . . . I get panicky about . . . ah, how I can handle it. Ah . . . I guess there is so much to understand and there is so much to deal with that I don't . . . I don't take the time to really think things out.

T: Can you describe that panicky feeling for me? What does it feel like to feel panicky?

H: I feel that I will make the wrong decision and I'll be stuck. That's what it boils down to . . . it's because I can't think about it. I feel I'm going to make a decision I'm going to regret. That's the way it manifests itself. It's like it's because I don't feel I have enough time. I seem to . . . ah . . . (his affect is more one of depression than of panic).

T: Wait. You said to me "When I do have time, Marshall, I feel panicky."

H: When I do think about it.

T: (I move in close to him to create an atmosphere of sharing and safeness.) What you're doing is obsessing. You're thinking so much, you're obsessing. Your thoughts go round and round.

H: Yeah.

T: You'll stay stuck as long as you obsess, because that energy goes nowhere. I'm going to try to help you move from obsessing from your head and feeling your deeper feelings. I want you to try to describe your feelings, not what you think. Describe to me what you feel. Try again. When you feel panicky, try to describe that feeling to me. . . . (Long pause. This is not a good question because I am asking him to describe a past feeling and he does not know how to do this.) Let's go another way. (I will concentrate on the present.) What are you feeling now. What are you experiencing now?

H: A little frustration because I can't express my feelings.

T: Can you describe in words what it feels like to experience frustration?

H: I think that's about it.

T: You're feeling stuck.

H: Uh, huh.

T: Is there a feeling of anger?

H: Dog–gone, I should be able to express myself. I'm always hard on myself. Of course there is a little anger.

T: How do you recognize the anger?

H: (Begins to use imagery.) Because it's like two boys, one saying "Come on," to the other. The little sensitive guy and the real tough guy. The tough guy is saying, "Come on, god damn it, you know what to say. You're the sensitive one. You can figure it out. It's your turn to talk," kind of thing. If you want to talk about how somebody feels. There's two conflicting . . . maybe not conflicting, but maybe not totally compatible.

The inner conflict is clearly visible in the imagery of the two boys, one saying, "Come on," to the other. The real tough guy and the little sensitive guy. I believe the "tough guy" represents the critical parent and the "sensitive little guy" is Gary, the child. I will attempt to stay with this imagery to help him define what his "little boy" is experiencing. How does the "sensitive guy" relate to the "tough guy?" Gary is a physically large, muscular man.

T: How does the sensitive guy respond to the tough guy?

H: He is saying leave me alone so that I can think about it.

T: How is the sensitive guy feeling as he is staying with the tough guy?

H: (Responding with a though statement.) I think he's feeling pressured.

T: Describe the pressure the little guy is feeling. Picture that sensitive guy.

H: (Again Gary responds with thought.) I think basically the way I am is I feel I have to respond and give a response that is satisfactory, that meets other people's expectations.

This is a major problem for Gary. He is so insecure he is constantly worried about people judging him.

T: So that sensitive guy is saying?

H: He wants to please... he wants to please... I want to please...

Gary is well aware of the submissive position he often takes, especially in his relationship with Nancy. By such supplication, he builds up resentment in himself and toward the person to whom he is submitting.

T: So that sensitive guy is not pleasing the tough guy?

H: Yeah, basically it boils down to, I don't because of my own value system. I don't belong in that situation. I guess I felt... ah... after leaving I felt frustrated because I felt that I was still misunderstood. I guess that's it. Not being understood.

Nearly three months of conjoint sessions with the couple had not changed Gary's opinion that Nancy cannot and will not understand how he thinks and feels.

H: ... And really being able to deal with it, and that's frustrating, nor having the energy to deal with it. I'm not sure Nancy really understood what I was trying to say. After we left she was really upset, so I asked. (This is new behavior. He would have normally withdrawn.) I guess I knew the way she felt. I just wanted to hear her say it. She asked me how I felt and I didn't know what to say. We did however

. . . I felt bad going back and listening to the tape. I guess the other thing is it really is hard to go back and listen. I don't necessarily feel totally relieved. But I feel better about it.

T: Why do you feel better?

H: Because I did it. (Was assertive and honest.) Part of what I was feeling was, like wow! I can't believe I really said that. Sometimes it's just that things really hurt and I close off. I guess it was really easy for me to understand why I did it after listening to it.

During subsequent sessions, Gary's confidence grows and he continues to express his feelings. He finally tells Nancy that he was ambivalent about their marriage from the beginning. However, even in overcoming the fear of expressing himself, Gary is not able to believe that Nancy will ever understand him. Nancy gives up the hope that she will ever be able to convince Gary that she loves him and that she is able to empathize with his pain. She decided not to wait for him to resolve his ambivalence and made a decision to divorce him. A few months later she filed for divorce, sold the house and returned to her hometown.

It is not uncommon for the spouse who initially wants to stay in the marriage to be the one to decide to leave. This happens because the partner is forced into examining the marriage for the first time. If there is a positive self image, as I believe to be true of Nancy, then the partner who was not ambivalent will recognize the hopelessness of the situation and take action to correct it. I believe in this case Gary had built up so much resentment over the years that it negated whatever love he might have had for Nancy. As a result he was not able to believe that she was sincere in her desire to love and understand him.

The case of Gary and Nancy demonstrates how individuation therapy can work with partners who are ambivalent about their marriage. In this case, individuation therapy was helpful in assisting Gary to understand and express his feelings to his wife and to his parents. As a result, it was possible to move into marital therapy. As is true in this case, the resolution of the ambiguity can sometimes lead to divorce or separation.

If spouses do not feel free in a marriage, they cannot be receptive to loving gestures. Instead, the experience a sense of obligation and the marriage becomes a burden rather than a relationship where there can be validation and enhancement.

18

ACCOMMODATION THERAPY: THE MARRIAGE OF CHESTER AND GEORGIA

ACCOMMODATION THERAPY was successfully used to assist Chester and Georgia to establish a peaceful and respectful relationship. Prior to therapy they were living with a marriage in which they verbally abused one another and continually argued both privately and publicly. Chester is a fifty–two year old dentist. Georgia, fifty, is the business manager of Chester's practice. The couple has been married for thirty years. They have five children. Only seventeen year old Terry is still in the home. They have few mutual friends, but Chester has a separate network of close relationships. Georgia has a few friends but relies primarily upon Chester for support and social activities. Both are non–practicing Catholics but they share strong religious beliefs. The couple met and fell in love while Chester was an undergraduate. Georgia worked outside the home and was the primary caretaker of the children while Chester completed his education.

The relationship began in a normal way. Both enjoyed their junior and senior years in college together. They married immediately upon graduation. Their dream was to have Chester complete dental school and establish a practice which would allow them to lead a comfortable life. They both wanted a large family. While dating, they treated each other with warmth and respect. They entered the marriage expecting to share a life of love. Unfortunately the enchantment phase of their marriage was brief and they did not make it past the negotiation phase of marital development.

Chester and Georgia were never able to successfully make the transition from being single to being married. Immediately following their marriage Chester began dental school, a move which required that he be away from home a great deal. After three months of marriage Georgia became pregnant with Lisa. The pregnancy had many complications. Consequently, before the couple had time to effectively adjust to married life, they were burdened with financial and emotional difficulties. After Lisa was born, there was additional stress for Georgia as she had to make time for her work, household duties and most of the parental responsibility. From the first year of the marriage Georgia began to have strong feelings of abandonment and overwhelming fatigue.

Chester felt burdened by the demands of dental school and what he felt were unrealistic demands for support from Georgia. Arguments frequently erupted and instead of feeling free to be themselves in a loving relationship, both felt burdened and trapped in an intolerable situation in which they perceived a future which promised only more responsibility and obligation.

As the years passed, the marriage continued to deteriorate. The establishment of Chester's successful dental practice was not enough to keep the marriage from further degeneration. The couple had considered divorce several times. They agreed to stay together out of religious mandate, social pressure and because of the children.

Chester was frequently involved in extra-marital affairs. Georgia knew about many of Chester's involvements. Both had become alcoholics. Although there was never any physical abuse, the couple often engaged in violent arguments. They had been asked by many restaurants to leave and never return because of their disruptive behavior. They seldom settled arguments and they continued to attack each other's dignity. There was profound mistrust which resulted in each trying to control the other's behaviors, feelings and thoughts. Both resented and blamed the other for the unhappiness in the marriage. In short, the couple had reached the abyss. As in the case of many such couples, they developed a pathological "we psyche" with neither able to exhibit much autonomy. To cope with his unhappiness, Chester turned to women and alcohol while Georgia tried to deal with the situation by compulsive drinking and shopping.

The couple was first seen in family therapy to deal with a specific issue: their daughter, Terry, had become anorexic. After applying structural family therapy to resolve Terry's problems, I turned my attention to the marital relationship. Chester was clear about the fact that he did not love his wife, but Georgia still loved Chester. She believed that if Chester would work on improving the relationship his love for her would return.

While talking separately with the spouses, I learned that Chester was involved in a long–term affair with a woman named Katie. Georgia suspected the infidelity but Chester denied any involvement. Georgia did not know that Chester was considering leaving her for Katie. Two weeks later, Chester moved out of his home to consider his decision. Following the move, the couple was seen in concurrent individuation therapy. The goal for Georgia was to help her overcome her alcoholism, her depression and her need to stay in an unfulfilling marriage. Treatment with Chester was aimed at examining his ambivalence about his marriage, understanding his relationship with Katie and improving his self–esteem.

Using primarily supportive and affective interventions, I was able to help Georgia stop her drinking, alleviate her depression and reaffirm her dignity. She joined Alcoholics Anonymous, developed a social support system and returned to church. She decided that she loved Chester enough to wait for his decision about continuing the marriage.

Katie was invited to therapy so that I could better assess her relationship with Chester. (Some therapists would be apprehensive about this intervention because it could be seen by Georgia as a betrayal of her trust. I believe however, that I am not responsible for the circumstances under which the marriage is operating and I must be free to do what is necessary to understand the situation.) Katie loved Chester, but had made the decision that if he did not divorce his wife she would not continue the relationship. She felt sad for Georgia but did not believe that she was responsible for the problems in the marriage. Although Chester said that he loved Katie he did not feel free to divorce Georgia. His primary reasons were that he could not hurt his children and that the Catholic Church prohibited divorce.

I decided to directly engage Chester's reasons for remaining in the marriage. I did not attempt to assess the legitimacy of his reasons by exploring his unconscious beliefs about them. The traditional therapeutic approach could take months. I believed that working directly would expedite the treatment process. This was accomplished by encouraging him to talk with his children and with a priest about a possible divorce. Such an approach would encourage Chester to address his beliefs, fears and concerns rationally rather than intellectually. If, after following my suggestions, he decided to remain in the marriage, it would be a decision that was internalized at a much more profound level.

Chester's children admitted that they would be happier if their parents were divorced and they assured Chester that they would continue to relate to him in a loving way. After talking with a priest and examining his conscience he came to the conclusion that even though there was a lot of unhappiness in the relationship, he believed in his heart that he was married to Georgia and therefore was not entitled to an annulment.

Having helped Chester internalize his commitment to Georgia, I proceeded to try to help him understand his deeper feelings regarding the relationship. He was able to recognize feelings of rejection, abandonment and loneliness. He also began to accept responsibility for his contribution to the unhappiness as well as the accomplishments of the marriage. As a couple they had raised five loving children, built a business which provided a vital service and established some close friendships.

Even after he came to realize that he could not end his marriage Chester could not bring himself to tell Katie. This situation allowed me to help him recognize his fears and insecurities and to learn how they impacted on his personal relationships, including his marriage. Katie realized that Chester was making no move toward initiating a divorce and ended the affair. Therapy then shifted to helping Chester deal with his loss. After several months of working on his grief and insecurities, Chester made a decision to return home.

Concurrent individuation therapy helped Chester and Georgia extricate themselves from the negative spiral, reclaim autonomy and establish dignity. By the time Chester returned home they had gained the maturity which would allow them to deal more objectively with their marriage. Conjoint therapy resumed and I introduced the idea of an accommodating marriage. Georgia was hesitant, but soon learned that she needed to begin accepting the truth about the relationship and part of the truth was that Chester did not love her. I worked directly with each spouse in conjoint session to share their pain associated with years of marital discord. I then had them share with each other the sadness, emptiness and feelings of inadequacy that they had experienced over the years. This provided a bridge between the two and provided a foundation on which they could build a friendship.

In subsequent sessions the couple established realistic expectation for the relationship. They began to speak to each other with truth and respect. The couple never did express joy or intimacy nor did they expect to find these feelings in the marriage. They recognized that much was missing but they were ready to accept a peaceful friendship. They agreed to increase their outside activities together, but they also continued to relate individually to their separate sets of friends. Treatment ended after fourteen months.

The sessions with Chester and Georgia are illustrative of the variety of interventions available to therapists. Among other stratagem, the therapist involved significant others, encouraged outside support for overcoming alcoholism, suggested specific clerical expertise and provided supportive affective and cognitive interventions when seeing the partners individually and conjointly.

19

ACCOMMODATION THERAPY: THE MARRIAGE OF GORDON AND SALLAH

THE PROCESS OF ESTABLISHING an accommodating marriage is very painful. For some couples it is very much like the experience of a divorce or a death. Accommodation is the death of hope. It is a giving up of any expectation of future enhancement and enrichment in the marriage. It is the death of the dream of sharing a joyful life with a happy partner. Spouses must mourn the end of the reasonable expectation that they will be loved and valued for themselves. There will also be the loss of taking pleasure in or being invested in the happiness of the partner.

An accommodating marriage is like Hungary after the occupation. The mindset is "This is not what we wanted, but we will have to live with it. The forces are too strong to fight. But we will not lose ourselves. We will do what we can, within this regime, to get our needs met. We will remain who we are but we will never really be happy. We have allowed a stranger to occupy our territory." The case of Gordon and Sallah is an example of the difficult road some couples must travel to arrive at a peaceful co-existence.

Gordon is a thirty-four year old mechanical engineer and Sallah a thirty year old homemaker. They were married after five months of dating in college. They both say that they were in love when they married. Sallah has a master's degree in economics but has postponed her career and does occasional substitute teaching. Sallah came to America from Egypt on a student visa. When she married Gordon she was able to get permanent residency status. After she became a citizen, she sent for her family. Her parents and aunts live within blocks of the couple. Gordon and Sallah have been married for ten years and have three children aged seven, five and four.

The couple experienced a short enhancement phase of marriage, but they began to argue within days of their wedding. They had each brought their own insecurities into the marriage and were thus unable to negotiate their many cultural and personal differences. Both are considerate and intelligent people. They are also complementary in that Gordon relates to the world in a very structured and cognitive way while Sallah is spontaneous and emotional. Gordon found Sallah's personality to be more and more unacceptable as the marriage progressed. Sallah felt that Gordon was nurturing prior to the marriage but had since stopped being supportive. She now describes him as insensitive, dogmatic and condescending.

From the inception of the marriage neither partner has been able to validate or accept the other. Instead they have been engaged in a ten year war to change the other. Therapy began with the couple deeply trapped in the negative spiral. The argued constantly and were hypercritical of each other. Gordon had struck Sallah on occasion. They were ineffective at problem solving most issues. They felt no security in the relationship and were not invested in meeting each other's emotional needs. Finally, each had come to experience deep resentment for the other.

Both related to their children with warmth and caring but they did not agree on child rearing practices. They are proud of their children who are sensitive and polite. The couple also has a shared commitment to the Bahai Church.

When they entered therapy the couple lacked autonomy and dignity in their relationship. They had become accustomed to acting and reacting to each other's thoughts and feelings. They felt discounted and resentful toward the other for their predicament. Initially, they indicated they still loved one another and divorce was not an option. The couple was seen for two years. Several months were spent unsuccessfully trying to stop the intense conflict which was illustrated graphically in the session. Unable to help the couple to relate in a non-combative way, the therapeutic approach was switched to conjoint individuation therapy.

Several months were required to finally stop the intense reactiveness and blaming. After a year of therapy they were still unable to accept each other's beliefs and behaviors. Therapy shifted back to having the couple problem solve issues associated with the children, finances and activities. Several contracts designed to resolve various issues were established, but all efforts failed. In the second year of treatment the therapist reintroduced the idea of an accommodation marriage, something the couple had earlier refused. Recognizing that little had changed, they agreed.

Gordon and Sallah wished to participate in concurrent accommodation therapy as they both believed they could not trust the other with the exposure of their private feelings. This fear had persisted throughout the marriage. The initial focus of therapy with Gordon was helping him give up the idea that he could get Sallah to agree to his demands and change her behavior. The goal was to get him to control his behavior by appealing to his logic. This was accomplished by using a cognitive restructuring intervention of continuously repeating the question "Why did he continue to try to change Sallah when years of effort had failed?" It took several months for him to finally give up his expectations of changing Sallah. In so doing, he began to recognize the primary feelings of helplessness and sadness. He recalled that he experienced such feelings in his childhood, but he was not able to make the connection between past and present feelings. His parents were divorced when he was eleven. Gordon described his father as rigid and insensitive. He remembered his mother as hysterical and intrusive. I believe that these were some of the factors that contributed to his rigid character structure and his inability to respond to expressions of emotion.

Following achievement of the first goal, therapy then focused on Gordon's examining his deeper feelings toward Sallah. He recognized that he did not love or trust her nor did he enjoy being with her, but he would not consider divorce because his religion stresses keeping the family together at all costs. A conjoint session was held at which time Gordon told Sallah exactly how he felt. Gordon finally decided that he was doing all he could to establish a peaceful marriage and that any changes would have to be initiated by Sallah. I accepted what Gordon was saying and agreed to see him monthly to keep him focused on developments in the marriage.

Treatment with Sallah was directed at helping her to accept that she could not force Gordon to change his feelings or behaviors. When Sallah finally began to see and accept Gordon's position, he informed her that he did not in any way love or respect her. He also told her that he perceived her emotional outbursts and expressions of love as manipulative attempts to control him and said that he doubted that she really loved him. Sallah heard his words, but did not internalize the meaning. She continued to block or deny what Gordon was saying. Using supportive and affective interventions, the therapist assisted Sallah in finally accepting Gordon's statements. The following interview illustrates a major turning point in treatment. Sallah comes to the realization that what she is experiencing is very much like mourning a death.

Following a brief discussion about the death of a close cousin, Sallah, in a very depressed posture, describes her present relationship with Gordon.

W: . . . I've been reading some of Kübler-Ross's books about the dying patient and as a result of that . . . you might have noticed . . . but I didn't . . . I have a dead relationship with my husband. It really, really hurts me . . . that all these years I denied the illness. I have denied the fact from the very beginning that this was not a healthy relationship and I have been angry about it and I think I've been in a state of shock ever since I've realized this. As I really had to face it with myself . . . I've been in physical shock. In the last few days I have lost three or four pounds. I have been very agitated . . . I don't want to resign myself to this . . . I would like to accept it. I woke up one night and saw Gordon and didn't recognize him . . .

I've been sharing this with my mother but I don't want to tell anyone else my feelings because everybody wants me to deny it because it's too horrible. Why don't you help me deny it?

I asked if he talked to you and he said yes . . . I asked him what did you two talk about. I don't know what got me to ask him but he said "What goes through your head when we have sex?" I said I used to think it was because you loved me but I don't want to fool myself anymore. Then he said that for him it was physical. He said he just did it to satisfy himself . . . and that made me feel in shock again. I must accept it but it really, really hurts. I thought I had accepted that he didn't love me but I guess I didn't . . . it's hard for me to let go of the relationship. I think part of me is dying.

T: (Pushing her to keep in touch with her primary feelings in order to facilitate the mourning process.) What does it feel like to be dying?

W: (After a pause.) I have to face it, right? I'm grieving, but I don't look at myself as a depressed person. I've lost weight. I feel tired . . . I'm fighting not to feel the pain. I feel . . . I feel angry . . . angry with me . . . angry because I feel incompetent . . . angry at my own behavior toward a bad situation . . . I'm feeling sad . . . I can't go back the way it was. It's too painful . . . I don't want to feel defeated anymore. I'm young. I want to expand myself. Like you've always been telling me . . . it's a new experience for me. I have to find myself for me . . . I have to look after me.

In the subsequent months Sallah becomes more depressed. This is manifested by weight loss, sleeplessness, tearfulness, lethargy, social withdrawal and a lack of sexual energy. I continue to use supportive and effective interventions. Sallah stops blaming Gordon for the problems in the marriage and accepts responsibility for contributing to the marital discord. In so doing she turns more inward and recognizes that she has given up dignity and autonomy, but is puzzled about her reasons for doing so. She is also puzzled by her poor self–esteem and the origin of her need to believe that the measure of a person (particularly herself) is determined by physical appearance, clothing, status and money.

Although she loves her parents, Sallah begins to realize how her family had contributed to her problems. For nearly 40 years her father had been verbally abusive and condescending to Sallah's mother and the mother gave in to all his demands. There were constant conflicts among family members and criticism of Sallah's appearance and accomplishments. She assumed the role of family peacemaker. Sallah had not been validated or accepted for herself in either her family of origin or her marriage. Her marriage mimicked her parents' relationship. Sallah was able to recognize that she had stayed in this dysfunctional marriage because it seemed normal to her. She never realized that she had an alternative.

As treatment progressed, Sallah began to be assertive with her parents, which created a more positive manner of interaction. An important change was that her mother began to recognize and be supportive of Sallah's depression and stopped suggesting that Sallah simply accept the state of the marriage. Additionally, Sallah began to develop her spiritual awareness. She stopped turning to Gordon to validate her. Instead, she began to accept herself for her numerous positive qualities. Finally even though she experienced great pain, she recognized that she was beginning to establish her autonomy, dignity and sense of freedom. She decided that she would pursue her dream of a degree in veterinary medicine.

At the present time Sallah plans to remain in the marriage. As she continues to grow and develop it is hard to predict what her final decision will be. In a recent interview Sallah said: "During the week I've realized that I am living with a stranger." Her observation is accurate. Neither has invited the partner to know each other, but instead they have each made demands to have their needs met. Such attitudes will only serve to keep them strangers.

Sallah has not completed the process of grieving. At times she hopes that the marriage will improve, but instead of demanding love she now invites Gordon to know her. Each time he rejects her she realizes further that she cannot expect what he cannot give. She has not yet fully established her dignity and autonomy. When she accomplishes these objectives, I will see the spouses in conjoint therapy to negotiate an accommodating marriage. I suspect because of the growth of the partners that they will be able to related as mature adults.

It is not uncommon for a couple to battle for years when the marriage contains the following characteristics: no mutual love, a relationship based on dependency, no change of a divorce or separation. To give up conflict in such cases the couple must come to the realization that they have lived for years in a marriage with little or no substance; they will probably spend the rest of their lives with a partner who will neither love or enhance them; they will have to accept responsibility for themselves. In short, they will be imprisoned in a marriage which will only perpetuate feelings of loneliness and isolation.

Most such couples never have the opportunity to learn that with assistance they might be able to establish a peaceful and comfortable marriage or failing that, might find peace by ending the marriage.

20

VERITIVE THERAPY: THE MARRIAGE OF ALAN AND CAROLEE

THE CASE OF ALAN AND CAROLEE describes the kind of misery couples can endure when they marry with little personal dignity and for the wrong reasons. Alan is a forty year old building contractor and Carolee is a thirty-eight year old attorney. They married after having known each other for one year in college. Alan was not sure he loved Carolee but he had felt comfortable with her. She was the only woman he had ever dated. Carolee claimed that she married Alan because she found him pathetic and felt sorry for him. They have been married for eighteen years and have four children ages eighteen, fourteen, twelve and ten. Both are involved in their church community which takes a negative attitude toward divorce, especially condemning divorced women.

The couple displayed extreme reactiveness from the beginning of therapy. They shouted accusations and counter-accusations. They stated that they fought constantly and could not come to any agreement about anything—children, money, or household tasks. They felt no trust in the other to care for their emotional or personal needs. Each felt enormous resentment toward the other. It was evident that the couple never reached the enchantment phase of marriage and that they were deeply caught in the negative spiral.

The circumstances under which the couple married doomed the relationship from the beginning. Alan stated in therapy that he was extremely insecure and that he married Carolee for support. He believed before they married that she did not possess the rigid, critical, demanding and dogmatic personality traits that she now displayed. Alan did not enter the marriage with the hope of having a loving relationship, but rather expected someone to meet his insecure needs. Such expectations establish a relationship based on taking rather than giving, upon obligation, not freedom and upon dependency needs rather than mutual nurturing. Alan's self-esteem was low before the marriage and the relationship served only to make him feel even more inadequate. As he was not free to be himself he was not free to give himself to Carolee.

I suspect that Carolee's feelings of "pity" for Alan were a projection of her own feelings of inadequacy. It is clear that she was so alienated from her own dignity that she allowed herself to marry someone she did not respect. When asked if she loved Alan she responded that she did not know the meaning of the word "love." In therapy, she told Alan that she found him to be pathetic, disgusting, inadequate, and crude. He minimized these attacks by such remarks as "She doesn't know what she is saying or she would leave the marriage." I believe that by marrying Alan under the guise of pity, Carolee could establish herself as the benevolent spouse and thereby establish a position of superiority over Alan. Implicit in the marital agreement would be the belief that Alan owed her something for her "generosity." The relationship, therefore, would be one not based upon sharing love but rather one based on obligation. When Alan did not fulfill his obligation by meeting her practical needs, Carolee became furious, believing herself to be the victim of a bad deal.

The negative spiral in which the couple was caught allowed for no autonomy and no manifestation of dignity. Essentially, the relationship was based on each spouse's wish to control the other. Neither was ready to take responsibility for their part in the marital discord.

All therapeutic efforts to help the couple to deal with their problems failed. Initially, the emphasis was on helping the couple to improve communication. I would, for example, have them listen to tape recordings of sessions and point out how they did not hear each other. They countered this intervention by stating that they did not believe what the other partner was saying. They were involved in reading and interpreting each other's thoughts. This kind of negative "mind reading" led to a profound distrust. They simply did not want to know each other's pain. Carolee stated that she was not interested in knowing how Alan was feeling, she just wanted him to change his behavior.

Both partners were from very dysfunctional families. Alan's parents were dogmatic and physically abusive. Carolee's parents were emotionally closed and rigid. Her father had an alcohol problem and was seldom home. Efforts to create autonomy by modeling family of origin therapy failed because both partners refused to recognize that such interventions might be helpful to the marriage. Various strategic interventions used to block negative circular patterns were not helpful in resolving any of the problems.

The couple refused to consider a divorce. Alan held that his religion forbade divorce. Carolee was mindful of the church's stand and also believed that she would be ostracized from her family and friends if she divorced.

The couple finally agreed to try to establish an accommodating marriage. At this point in treatment Carolee refused to be seen conjointly. I acquiesced to her request as I believed that further conjoint sessions would prove disruptive. The couple could not get beyond constant criticism of each other in conjoint session. Emphasis in the concurrent individuation sessions focused upon helping each spouse to take responsibility for their part in the marital discord and to see what each was willing to do to improve the relationship.

Alan made some effort toward change but he believed that Carolee would undermine his efforts. Attempts to have him talk about himself failed. He could not think about himself without thinking about his wife. Their identities were so tied together that neither had much sense of self. I then shifted to veritive therapy in an attempt to help Alan recognize the destructive aspects of the marriage and the negative way that Carolee perceived him. Alan's insecurities made it impossible for him to accept how much his wife demeaned him and how little happiness he was getting out of the marriage. He rationalized, minimized, denied, blocked and distorted the issues I presented to him.

It became evident that Carolee's suggestion to have me see Alan separately was an effort to enlist my help in changing Alan's behavior. Carolee continued to refuse to take any responsibility for the problems in the marriage. She eventually admitted to me that she knew that if she did not cooperate by participating in concurrent therapy Alan would see her as the problem and would withdraw from treatment. After hearing her reasons for being there, I proceeded with veritive therapy. I confronted her with what I believed to be the problems in the relationship. She continued to refuse to recognize that she had any responsibility for the problems.

For the last session, I saw the couple conjointly. I once more confronted them with my view of the situation and what I believed was necessary if they were to achieve a truce. I then told them that I believed that I could no longer help them and that I was excusing myself from working with them. I gave them the names of other therapists they could chose from if they felt that more therapy would be helpful. They agreed that therapy was not helping and we terminated.

Alan and Carolee's marriage was a desperately unhappy one because it lacked any substance. When they married they did so out of insecurity and not love. The relationship served to alienate them further from their dignity and they lost much of their autonomy. Instead of having a marriage based on freedom and growth they established one on a muddy foundation of control, negation and interdependence. This led to a loss of self and imprisoned them in a circular pattern of misery. They will not give up a marriage in which there is no hope and much despair.

21

VERITIVE THERAPY: THE MARRIAGE OF NED AND PHYLLIS

A MARRIAGE THAT IS BASED on mutual love facilitates the development of a "we psyche," which leads to mutual enhancement. Conversely, a marriage based primarily on a sense of duty and dependency needs encourages a "we psyche" which leads to a loss of autonomy and profound unhappiness. The case of Ned and Phyllis demonstrates the anguish spouses experience when they cannot overcome resentments which have built up for years.

Ned is a 55 year old chiropractor and Phyllis a 53 year old city college instructor. The couple has been married for twelve years. Phyllis' three children from a previous marriage had lived with them but all have left the house. Phyllis' first marriage lasted ten years. She married Ned after dating him for five years after her divorce. She had been comfortable with the relationship as it was, and felt that Ned pressured her into marriage. Phyllis was apprehensive in marrying Ned as she had had a conflictual first marriage. Ned had been helpful in encouraging her to leave the first marriage by providing friendship and support. They became lovers after her divorce.

The couple agree they had been happy together before the marriage. They had many shared activities and they were both involved with Phyllis's children. Ned wanted to get married and pressured Phyllis for years. She condescended only after Ned threatened to end the relationship if she did not marry him. Phyllis believed that he pressured her at a vulnerable time as she had been recovering from surgery and needed his emotional support. She agreed to his demand even though it was not clear to her that she loved him.

Shortly after the marriage, Phyllis began to experience severe episodes of depression, which she attributed to unhappiness in the marriage. The problems initially centered around the children. Ned and Phyllis continually argued about expectations for behavior and responsibility for caretaking. As the children entered adolescence they began to exhibit severe oppositional behavior. They became involved with drugs and illegal activities. As young adults, all were functioning at a marginal level.

Initially, Phyllis entered treatment alone. She indicated that Ned refused to participate in marital therapy. The couple never went beyond the negotiation phase of marital development and were very deep in the negative spiral. Phyllis regretted marrying Ned. In many ways the couple were living separate lives. As she was unhappy in her marriage, Phyllis developed professional and personal interests outside the home. Ned opposed her outside activities because he believed that they did nothing to make his wife any happier. He also realized that she was distancing herself from him. When they were together, they seldom spoke and they were unhappy. If they did speak, the conversation ended in a disagreement. Both felt misunderstood and victimized. Neither accepted responsibility for contributing to the marital discord and each blamed the other for all the problems.

Therapy with Phyllis focused on job related problems and her ambivalence about continuing in the marriage. She strongly believed that she was trapped in the relationship. Her religion to which she had strong ties, discouraged divorce under any circumstances. She also had the burden of not wanting to disappoint her aged parents with another divorce. She felt that divorcing again would make her a "two time loser," Finally, she believed that Ned might attempt suicide if she left and she understandably did not want to be responsible for his death.

Initially, therapy focused on problem solving issues associated with her work. She eventually decided to change to a new school district. Cognitive, affective and supportive interventions were used to examine her thoughts and feelings associated with marriage. She refused to discuss her problems with her parents, feeling that it would only cause them pain. It became apparent that Phyllis was aware of her marital situation and knew how much pain she would experience if she was to remain in the marriage. I chose veritive therapy, emphasizing her dilemma. I shared with her my belief that her problems were situational and that she would face pain no matter what her decision. I kept reinforcing the idea that the pain would not go away if the relationship did not change and that it did not look like that was going to happen. As she began to accept the hopelessness of the situation she began to change her position and began to think about ending the marriage. She developed a plan for leaving. The plan involved moving to another part of the state. She went so far as to accept an interview at a city college in her target area.

When Ned was informed of Phyllis' plans, he became hysterical and threatened suicide. He indicated that he would now do anything to keep the marriage together, even begin marital therapy. Phyllis felt sorry for Ned, was frightened by his suicidal threats, and believed that marital therapy could help the marriage. She decided to stay in the relationship.

In the first marital session, Ned indicated that he was only there at Phyllis' insistence and that he did not believe therapy would be helpful. He was doing it for Phyllis, not himself. He also indicated that he did not believe in divorce because of his religion. I was not able to help the couple to problem solve or to improve their communication. There was profound mistrust and resentment and neither spouse was willing to take any responsibility for the disharmony in the marriage. They did not trust what the other was saying. They mind-read, discounted, and did not believe any positive intent behind any spoken statement.

My efforts to build bridges, create a positive atmosphere in which change could occur, and avoid non-negotiable issues all failed. Each spouse continued to believe that the other was self-centered, insensitive and rigid.

It appeared to me that although this couple lived together, they were emotionally divorced. Neither was interested in knowing how the other felt or cared about what his/her partner believed. Each was convinced the other needed to change if the marriage was to improve.

Ned withdrew from therapy after three months. It was clear to him therapy was not helping the marriage. This made him more helpless and discouraged. I was hoping that his greater feelings of helplessness might serve to initiate a change which might help the marriage or move to end it. In this case, by withdrawing from treatment, Ned diffused the intensity associated with the helplessness of the situation. Thus, the crisis I was hoping for never materialized. When I called Ned to formally end with him, he thanked me for my efforts. He stated that he hoped someday Phyllis might change.

I continued to see Phyllis in veritive therapy. At this time, however, Phyllis decided to remain in the marriage even though she could see no sign of change. She believed her new job and her outside interests would help her to "tolerate her marriage." I ended therapy, wishing them both the best of luck. A one year follow–up call revealed the couple was still together and there had been no change in the relationship.

The decision Ned and Phyllis made to remain together even though they were both miserable was not surprising to me. When Phyllis entered therapy she was in a state of crisis, even though she was not seriously considering ending the marriage. Individuals in crisis are very open to change. Veritive therapy served to amplify her interpersonal crisis. Seeing the hopelessness of the situation and being in a position where she was susceptible to change, she began to consider leaving the relationship. Her crisis was diffused when Ned threatened suicide and also offered the possibility he might change. Marital therapy was not effective in creating a hope for change. In the meantime, by accepting a new local teaching position, Phyllis lost her opportunity to physically move away from Ned. The crisis was further diffused when Phyllis discovered that she really enjoyed her new job. She no longer felt the acute pain associated with the marriage. Ned, on the other hand, had no intention of leaving the marriage, no matter how unhappy he might be. He would rather be unhappy with Phyllis than live without her.

The case of Ned and Phyllis is one more example of a marriage which started off on a bad foundation. Phyllis did not enter the marriage freely, but was coerced into saying yes at a time when she was vulnerable. She never took any responsibility for her part of the unhappiness but continued to blame Ned. She was never invested in nurturing, validating or knowing him, nor was she receptive to his overtures of love. Step–parenting issues further complicated the marriage.

They quickly developed a circular pattern of interaction which led them deep into the negative spiral.

All efforts at helping this couple improve their relationship failed. I have a responsibility to respect their right to live their lives as they wish and so I decided to end treatment. It is possible that in the future this couple will be receptive to change and will return to therapy. But for now they have chosen to continue to be unhappy.

22

DIVORCE THERAPY: THE MARRIAGE OF SAALAM AND LIZ

MOST COUPLES BEGIN MARRIAGE with the hope of sharing love and living a life of happiness. There are few marriages where partners do not experience moments of happiness, share difficult times and develop a network of social relationships. The divorce process breaks apart this "we psyche," disrupting every area of life that has come to feel normal and natural. There is the additional pain that there will be no fulfillment of mutual dreams. Finally, there is the fear of an uncertain future. Divorce is, for most people, one of life's most devastating experiences.

Saalam and Liz entered marital therapy in an effort to reconcile differences and rebuild a happy marriage. Shortly after beginning, Liz expressed ambivalence about the relationship and requested to be seen alone. In individuation therapy, she decided to end the marriage. The therapist assisted in helping her decide how to tell her husband and in examining how the husband might respond to her decision. Issues included understanding the stages of divorce, what to tell family members, and the frightening possibility that Saalam might threaten suicide.

Saalam, 30, is a mechanical engineer. He had immigrated to America from Turkey with his family of origin three years prior to marrying Liz. Liz, 28, is a high school math teacher. They met in college and had been married for five years. The couple has a three year old daughter, Hope.

Saalam and Liz began to have problems shortly after marriage when

Liz learned what expectations Saalam had regarding her relationship to his large extended family. Throughout the marriage most arguments centered around their involvement with his family. She had always felt his loyalty was centered around his family and not her.

In the following session a skillful therapist directs a session with this couple. She remains in control of the situation, is neutral, and is attentive to the pain of both partners. This session also exemplifies a lot of issues that are presented in divorce therapy. The session is permeated with tremendous sadness.

> *T:* I talked with you individually about why we should meet today. When you first started coming here you wanted to work on the marriage. Then Liz said that she needed a couple of weeks to work things out. It sounds like a decision has been made . . . and . . . ah, I thought it was important for us to get together and talk it over and . . . ah . . . talk about what it meant for the two of you . . . Ah, I talked with Saalam on the phone and he told me about the conversation over the weekend that you had also talked about. Ah, I was sensing that, Saalam, that you were feeling that Liz had said to you that the relationship was over but there was still some confusion for you. Is that true?
>
> *H:* When?
>
> *T:* When I talked with you this afternoon.
>
> *H:* There is no confusion . . . it's . . . ah . . . I feel bad all this time went by without me knowing I was doing something wrong.

As is normal, he is blocking all the years of complaining from Liz. He only hears her when she threatens to end the marriage. Recognizing the denial process, the therapist responds.

> *T:* Okay, I guess that you're experiencing that it's hard to believe that—that Liz was so unhappy—that there were problems and you didn't notice them. (She does not judge or criticize him but validates his view and thereby gives him emotional support.)
>
> *H:* Yeah.
>
> *T:* Okay, ah . . . (To facilitate the grief process.) How are you feeling about that?
>
> *H:* (After taking a deep breath.) I feel pretty bad.

T: Yeah.

H: Ah . . . I feel guilty or bad or things . . . ah, (He becomes a little incoherent) . . . we always had somebody at the house . . . and I think that was one of the problems.

(A short time later.)

T: I was sensing that Liz has told you she wants a divorce at this point, but you were feeling that you wanted another chance at it. Is that right?

H: Oh, yeah, absolutely . . . I . . . I . . . do feel, ah . . . we had a good time together and we have . . . ah . . . so far we have a very good family . . . we have a wonderful baby, so far . . . and I do like to get another chance, if possible, and what I was telling you . . . it is never too late . . . that's my side.

T: Have you asked Liz about that?

H: I didn't but . . . ah . . . I wasn't sure and I get a negative answer from her and I was a little confused.

T: Why don't you ask her and see if she can clarify it for you?

It is important that Liz talk with Saalam so that she can reaffirm her position and deal with his pain and her feelings about his pain. She also needs to keep repeating that it is over until he finally accepts the reality of her decision.

H: I did ask her.

T: Liz, were you hearing that? He understood what you said but he was asking for another chance. What are you feeling about that and why don't you let him know?

W: What did I say to you last night?

H: I don't understand. What time last night? I guess you said you put up with it for four years. (Meaning the extended family issue.) You have to remember this was the first time you told me I was doing something wrong . . .

W: The first time you heard it.

H: Okay, that's what I'm trying to say.

W: No . . . it's too late for me.

H: I'm sorry to hear that, because I was hoping you would give me another shot . . . 'cause I still love you very much.

W: I know you do.

H: I still want you back.

W: I think it will be better this way.

H: Why do you think it will be better this way?

W: Being . . . ah . . . I wouldn't say easier, but it would be better for me . . . ah . . . just to go out and do things my way now.

H: Why can't it be together?

W: No . . . I've tried . . . and I'm very tired of trying. It's been way too long.

T: Ah, Saalam, what I'm hearing is that it's hard for you to understand right now and accept what Liz is saying. That doesn't make a lot of sense to you. (That statement supports his pain. She follows with trying to get him to hear Liz.) But can you hear what Liz is saying about your relationship?

H: Why don't you repeat it again?

T: Okay, did you hear what she just said?

H: She said a lot of things.

W: Did you hear me say "It's over?"

H: Yeah.

W: Okay.

T: All right. I guess that really is hard for you to hear and to understand.

H: I'm sorry to hear that. I honestly did not expect to hear that.

T: Yes. It comes as a real surprise to you. Kind of a shock.

H: . . . My heart has been getting in knots. I . . . ah . . . I'm bleeding pretty bad so are you sure you don't want to try?

W: Yes. I'm sure.

H: You've thought it out?

W: Right now I'm feeling sorry for you and that's no reason to try.

H: You don't want to give it one more time?

W: (Shakes her head no.)

T: (Moving to support Saalam.) Where does that come from? And you said that you were feeling sorry for Saalam.

W: Because it's taken him all this time to realize what was going on. He only found out Monday. And he's hurting very badly from it. At the same time he's trying to blame me for not being able to tell him the right way.

T: I'm wondering too, ah . . . when we spoke and you talked about being worried about Saalam . . . there sounds like there is some real concern on your part about his well–being and his happiness. Is that true?

W: That's there, oh yeah.

T: I guess even though you're concerned about Saalam that won't make the marriage work.

W: That's not enough.

T: Yeah ... and the pity and being sorry about him is not enough. How are you feeling?

W: A little surprised. I thought he understood Monday. I don't like to hear him beg because I know how desperate he is to put it that way.

T: Are you feeling desperate?

H: I'm not sure what you mean by desperate.

W: For us to get back together.

H: Yes.

W: I don't like to hear that. For anyone to swallow their pride. But it's been going on for too long.

T: So even though there is pain for you about how Saalam is feeling, it's still not enough for you to be able to try to make a go of your marriage again?

H: How can you make a big decision like that in a matter of a moment?

W: That decision has not been made in a moment. It's been made over a period of time. Only confirmed this past month. That this is the way for me to go.

H: Are you sure you are doing the right thing?

W: I'll never be sure. But this is what I want now. It's not an overnight decision.

H: Okay.

T: (After a pause.) This is really hard to hear.

H: All right. (He begins to leave.)

T: I'd like to talk just a couple of minutes. It just sounds like the decision has been made and the relationship or the marriage is over ... and it seems at this point that ... maybe I can help the two of you be seeing you individually and help you through this difficult time. This is not an easy time. It's very, very difficult and painful. Ah, it sound like Liz has been thinking about it for a long time, and Saalam, you have been very surprised by this now and it might be helpful for you to talk with me to sort through some of the things that ... that you are experiencing right now and also for you, Liz. I think we talked about this last week. I think, Liz, that you have decided to come individually.

W: Yes.

T: Okay. And I can go over this with you, as well as with Saalam.

H: Yes, but I would like to change the date.

T: Okay. You're both going through some really hard times and probably right now it feels overwhelming and really miserable for you. A lot of people feel like it's the end of the world and it can feel that way. (She had normalized their feeling and now offers hope.) . . . Ah . . . even though it feels that way . . . it doesn't have to be that way. And we can talk about it . . . sort through things and in time things will get better. Liz, what are you feeling right now?

W: I just want to know what you (Saalam) are feeling right now.

H: Pretty bad. If I had a gun I would shoot myself. (It is not uncommon for divorcing spouses to feel suicidal.) . . . I don't feel like I had enough chances for me to know something was wrong. I tell you now and I'll tell you again and again . . . I'm worried for what's happened.

T: (To Liz.) What are you feeling right now?

W: I'm sorry he's feeling that way.

T: About what?

W: I'm sorry he's feeling all of it. I'm sorry it had to come to this . . . I'm still not sure you understand why it had to come to this.

H: I do.

W: No, you don't. Not if you said it was five crummy years. It was a gradual thing.

T: Was it all crummy for you Liz?

W: No.

T: I kind of figured that because people don't stay together for five years if there weren't some good things going on. But I guess there wasn't enough to keep you there. What are your reactions to what he said about killing himself?

W: I don't think he really wants to do that.

T: Is that true, Saalam?

H: I do very much.

T: You feel like you would like to die right now. You love some people so much. And you don't want to live without her.

W: What about you? You're not being fair to yourself. Don't run away from your problems.

H: If you don't want me to run away from my problems, why don't you give me a chance to fix the problem? (He's bargaining.) You know it could be fixed.

W: I mean face it. Face the problem.

H: That's what I'm trying to do. Face the problem . . . I cannot do it by myself.

W: When you face problems you have to do it by yourself . . . I don't want you to hate me.

H: I don't hate you—there's no reason to hate you.

W: I just can see it turning.

H: Why? There's no reason. I still love you and I like you very much. Why do you feel that way?

W: I think that's what's going to come out of this.

H: You think I want you to come over to the house and get back together and we run through the same problems over and over and they get worse and worse. No. I don't want it. There is no reason . . . there is no reason . . .

W: Good.

H: I do care about you. Don't think that way, all right?

W: Then take care of yourself.

H: I will.

T: (Moving to have Saalam accept Liz's decision at a deeper level.) Saalam, can you really hear that Liz cares about you and doesn't want you to be hurt and wants you to pull through this okay? That's really there. Can you hear that? Can you accept that although there's not enough to keep her there with you now? Or can you at least hear that now?

H: I can hear it.

T: You guys have had five years of life together, you know, and it's had some problems but there was a lot of caring, too. And it's really sad sometimes that that's not enough to keep people together. It may not make a lot of sense. Sometimes people love each other a lot, but just can't make it as man and wife. That happens sometimes. That sounds to me like what happened here. You both care about each other. You're concerned. You want things to be good for Liz, Saalam, and Liz, you want Saalam to have a good life, too. You want him to be okay . . . and given a little time, the hurt will go away. It won't be nearly so painful as now. I've seen it happen a lot. It seems as if it's so painful that the pain will never go away. But life goes on and it will go away. It just takes time to go through. Okay, I'd like to stop now.

The therapist concludes by seeing the spouses alone. She evaluates Saalam's feelings of suicide and feels comfortable that he will not act on those feelings. Saalam indicates that he will have to live for his daughter. The therapist works effectively to facilitate the grief process.

The therapist recognizes the tremendous pain both spouses are feeling and moves to support them. At the same time, she encourages Liz to stand behind her decision to leave Saalam, while she (the therapist) helps him to accept it. She also builds bridges and validates the positive feelings they have for one another. She takes Saalam's suicidal thoughts seriously until she feels comfortable that he will not act on them. Finally, she normalizes the couple's feelings while offering them hope for the future. Thus, she creates an atmosphere in which both can heal and move on with their lives.

Saalam's responses to Liz are not unusual in such situations. Liz is further along in the divorce process because it was she who made the decision to leave. For Saalam, it is the first time he has really heard his wife threaten to leave him. When he finally hears her, he tries to negotiate for another chance. When she says no, he feels suicidal. In some cases, this kind of threat will draw a spouse back into the marriage. In this case, Liz supports Saalam's pain, but refuses to be intimidated back into the marriage. Liz's support helps Saalam save face and thereby encourages him to think of a future for himself apart from Liz. This creates further autonomy for her and initiates autonomy for him. He must learn to be responsible for himself.

The interaction between Saalam and Liz indicates that they are coping with the divorce process in the best possible way. Neither blamed the other, but instead, each is concerned about the well-being of the partner. With the assistance of the therapist, they are focusing upon the real issue, that of dealing with the pain associated with an impending divorce. If they continue in this manner, they will maintain their dignity and autonomy and bring an appropriate end to the marriage. They will also not carry unresolved issues into future relationships.

23

DIVORCE THERAPY: THE MARRIAGE OF MATTHEW AND JOSEPHINE

AS HAS BEEN PREVIOUSLY STATED, marriages that are entered into without mutual love are not conducive to the development of a covenant relationship. Couples will sometimes spend years trying to "make the relationship work." They will attempt to accept differences, make changes for their partner, and forgive past hurts. But, without love, certain dynamics are not possible. One cannot, for example, experience joy in wanting to know and enhance a spouse one does not love. It is not possible to know the kind of trust which allows one to invite another to know the inner recesses of the heart and to acknowledge and validate the essence of the other. The "silver cord" of intimacy will become too fragile to sustain the relationship or too rigid to allow movement.

The case of Matthew and Josephine is an example of a couple whose marriage begins without mutual love. They make a heroic effort to find happiness in the relationship. They do everything that they understand to be important for a successful marriage. They attempt to communicate openly and honestly. The accept differences and make the reasonable changes that are asked of them. But they fail to recognize the faulty construction upon which the marriage was built. Consequently, all attempts to build on that weak foundation cannot repair the intrinsic structural flaw. All their honest efforts fail.

Matthew, 28, is a concert pianist and Josephine, 28, is a biologist. They have been married for four years and have no children. They met and married in college. Josephine had an extensive dating history but had never felt love. She felt she lacked a capacity for love. She found Matthew more desirable than anyone she had previously known, but still did not have feelings she could describe as "being in love." She married him in the belief that the marriage could develop into a loving relationship. Matthew clearly felt love for Josephine and did not know that she had married him without reciprocal loving feelings.

Excerpts from the following session give evidence of the struggles of couples who marry without sharing love. It also demonstrates how a therapist facilitates and allows the painful process of grieving to take place. The grieving will allow the couple to disengage in an emotionally healthy way.

T: Why don't you bring me up to date on the facts?
W: Okay.
T: Tell me about your situation.
W: I'll start.
T: All right.
W: I'm not sure how the things came up again . . . I had said to you when I saw you on Wednesday that I wanted to schedule an appointment to tell Matthew I wanted a divorce and that I don't want to live with him any longer . . . and . . . ah . . . I wanted it to be more divorce therapy then . . . so that both had a chance to . . . to see what was going on with us . . . I have been very uncomfortable at home because I had this secret and I've been feeling really sick to my stomach . . . I wanted to share with you (Matthew) yesterday, I didn't want to live with you anymore . . . that I had made a decision. I don't think it was fair to keep stringing you along thinking Monday might be a remedial session to help the marriage.
H: I don't think you would have told me if I hadn't brought it up. (A short time later.)
T: So you got sick to your stomach and you wanted to share this with Matthew?
H: . . . I was proceeding on the basis that everything was going to be okay. She then told me she was no longer operating on that assumption. I asked her what was going on.
T: How did you take it?

H: Ah . . . like I share with you earlier, my gut feeling was that was what was going to happen. Ah . . . I felt pretty sad . . .

T: You're still feeling that way?

H: Yeah. I feel pretty much the same. As I said the other day, I just sat there and felt pretty sad, confused, hurt and angry. More angry than before.

T: More angry than before . . . I hear that in your tone of voice. What do you want to do this morning in this session? What do you want to talk about or address?

H: I want to know why you (Josephine) don't love me anymore. I feel deceived and that you weren't being honest with me. I feel that's what's happened since March or April or whenever it was you were saying in our session—you were saying you weren't happy and if things didn't get better you didn't want to stay married anymore. I felt that between then and now I haven't had any notice or warning or you haven't shared with me explicitly that you weren't . . . that you didn't feel you didn't love me anymore or your feelings were changing. I feel as if I've been served a "fait accompli"—that here it is—you know with . . . it's been like a bombshell going off. I don't like that at all. I feel really hurt and I don't know what's been going on . . . not that I could change it . . . but at least I could . . . would know where I stood . . . rather that your just saying here "I don't love you anymore and I don't want to live with you and I want a divorce."

T: So you . . .

H: I feel angry. I feel real hurt and real deceived. I don't think you treated me fairly. (These are normal feelings given the fact that he believes Josephine didn't keep him abreast of what she was honestly experiencing.)

T: What do you hear him saying?

W: That he wished I had shared with him what was going on. I though I had. I though that in the session we had with Tom I said to you "I didn't feel toward you the way you felt toward me."

T: What else did you hear him say?

(A short time later.)

T: You want to know what happened?

H: (Becoming tearful.) . . . Yeah, I feel really confused and I don't understand what's happened and ah . . . what's the basic reason you want to do what you want to do. I don't understand why.

People think that if they understand the "whys" the pain will go away—but it doesn't. The therapist recognizes that understanding the reasons why the marriage failed is not of primary importance, and that it is the dialogue that takes place which will free the couple. He therefore encourages the dialogue.

> *T:* It's really important that Josephine tell you about that. What do you want to do in this morning's session Josephine?
> *W:* I want the opportunity to share with Matthew feelings I have about not staying married to him . . . and some of the reasons that I don't stay married any longer, besides the reason that I don't love him. I'm not sure I ever loved you. I don't know, that when I think back on why I married you . . . I'm not sure that I loved you. I know I cared about you, and cared about you very deeply, but I don't know if I ever loved you . . . and I've known for a long time that I wasn't in love with you. I didn't know how to share that with you. One of the reasons I have is that it is very hard to live with someone who . . . to live with you when all you are is nice all the time. What I experience with you is that that's fake. I have a hard time having feelings about you when I experience you being gentle. When I act like an asshole and you pretend everything is nice and okay I feel frustrated. I feel all the time that I'm a jerk and I'm the bad guy in this relationship from the beginning.

Although this has been an issue throughout the marriage that has distanced the couple, the real issue remains that Josephine was never in love with Matthew. Couple believe that if they can fix the problems in the marriage that love will come. The issue is often stated as "if s/he would only change "that" I might love him/her. Couples fail to recognize that love allows for the true acceptance of the other person and that acceptance cannot be conditional.

> *T:* So you feel like a jerk, Josephine?
> *W:* I feel like I'm a quitter and that I should hang in there and really endure . . . and . . . and . . . ah . . . I feel like a heel . . . I feel like a heel for leaving such a nice person.
> *H:* . . . I thought I made a lot of growth in sharing how I really feel . . . I've been telling you I've been feeling happy or sad or whatever I'm feeling. And I guess you don't feel that way or you would see that.

Matthew believed that if he made the necessary changes that Josephine would love him. He then feels betrayed because he has made the necessary changes and he is still not loved.

>   *T:* You believe that you have made changes, but that somehow Josephine has not seen them?
>   (A short time later.)
>   *H:* I made a lot of changes. I thought they were necessary changes. And . . . ah, I feel like it hasn't done any good. And I didn't . . . ah and I'm not sure this is even true, but even if I did start a lot of those changes out of pleasing Josephine, I don't feel that way anymore. I was doing it for myself . . .
>   *W:* I didn't change to please you.
>   *H:* . . . One thing we shared . . . our marriage started off real lousy but I thought we both worked pretty hard to change that and to put it on a solid footing. I thought we had. I guess you didn't feel that way . . .
>   *T:* You said this came as a big surprise, that there was no warning.
>   *H:* I never knew Jo was not in love with me or that she was losing loving feelings.
>   *T:* Do you want to talk with Jo about that? It's a good question you're asking. "Why don't you love me? I thought I made some changes. I thought I was making myself more attractive for you and you didn't see the changes."
>   *H:* You never had the guts to share that with me earlier? Thanks. That's really a cop out. It really hurts.
>   *T:* How do you see that Josephine?
>   (A short time later.)
>   *W:* I showed you in lots of ways that I didn't care. You didn't want to see them. I haven't wanted to make love to you in the last two years. I've been distant emotionally. I've been picking on you. One of the things that's really hard for me is seeing you work so hard to change and wanting to make changes and me not giving a fuck whether or not you made changes, knowing deep inside it wouldn't make any difference. I did not yet have the courage to share that.

Although these statements are hard for Matthew to hear, they are necessary. Josephine is now being honest with herself and with him. In so doing, she gives him a direct message that the relationship must end and that it is not his fault. That it is simply what she feels and believes.

> *T:* What do you think of what Josephine said?
> *H:* I hear that she feels like a jerk and a quitter. I feel like you gave me a lot of signs and I didn't see them.
> *T:* How are you feeling now?

The therapist is trying to move the spouses from talking about issues and feelings to sharing their feelings.

> *H:* I feel that when we talked about not making love I wanted to know what was going on.
> *W:* I've been afraid to share my honest feelings. I kept thinking there was something wrong with me. (She begins crying openly.) You're a really nice person. I keep questioning what's wrong with me that I can't develop interest in this person who is working his ass off over here and who is really pleasant. But I don't! . . . and I don't know what to do about that. I don't want to live in a relationship with a person I feel is my best friend. I don't think that's fair and I don't think it's fair to you any more than it's fair to me to watch you work and to make changes and stuff and having me always picking on you.
> *H:* I never felt I wasn't getting anything back . . . (Matthew moves back into the role of being the supportive person, but Josephine challenges him.)
> *W:* I don't see how you could think that you were getting something back. I can count how many times we've made love in the last two years on one hand. I told you a bunch of times how I liked it when you were gone. What did you think I was saying?
> *H:* I'm not sure . . . maybe I was putting my head in the sand. Maybe I wasn't perceptive about what was happening.
> *W:* And I wasn't straight with you.
> (A short time later.)
> *H:* I feel dumb. I felt Josephine loved me and she didn't and that hurts. I feel stupid and it makes me wonder if I knew what it was in the first place.
> *T:* About being loved?
> *H:* I feel real confused about a lot of things. It really hurts. I thought I had a lot of good spots and we had good times.
> *W:* We had some good times. There were things that were good.

H: I feel like I'm being condemned for being a nice guy. (He is doubting his self–worth because of the rejection by Josephine.)

(A short time later.)

H: . . . I said to myself there were things I didn't like about you but there are more things about the way you are that I do like. And I said to myself that I accept the whole Josephine even though there are things about you that I don't like . . . and I don't think they're ever going to change but I'm satisfied with what I have because I felt the good outweighs the bad . . . (Matthew can make these statements because he loves Josephine.)

(Later.)

W: . . . Being in a stable relationship is okay with me and that wasn't true about me in the past. It's not the stability of our relationship that I'm having problems with.

H: What's the problem?

W: One of the problems is that I don't love you. The other problem—that I see as the biggest one, is that I don't want to be married to someone who is gone all the time . . . all that is small stuff. I just don't have loving feelings for you. I don't think that my going on tells you the other stuff is important.

T: You said, Matthew, that when Josephine tells you she doesn't love you, you don't know what that means.

H: I feel really hurt because Josephine says she doesn't love me the way I am. I don't know what else to say . . . I thought you cared about me and you don't.

W: Caring about you and loving you are two different things. I care about you very much.

H: . . . I thought you loved me but you say you don't. I feel that is a real rejection. Not rejection, that's not accurate. I feel like I've been run over by a steamroller. I feel like I have to leave our home which I really don't want to do. That's really important to me. I feel this is the beginning of a chain of events I don't want to face and I have to. I don't like that . . . I feel scared with my new contract . . . that I won't make enough money. I don't want to feel like I don't have anything . . . I don't want to be divorced! I want you to love. It's hard for me to believe you don't . . . I don't want to be divorced! I love you very much. I love our cats! I love our furniture!

(Matthew has become increasingly distraught throughout the session. He finally breaks down and cries hysterically.)

H: . . . I really feel alone. I'm losing the person I really care about.

Josephine tries to be supportive and then she breaks down and also begins crying. She makes encouraging statements. The crying continues and Matthew becomes incoherent. He is at last experiencing the hopelessness of the situation.

> *W:* I wish there was something I could do to make it better. . .
>
> *T:* This is the time where you can't take care of Matthew.
>
> *W:* (Tearfully.) I just want to make everything all right. I feel like the biggest jerk in the world because it's all my fault. Your life is going to be miserable because of me and I hate that feeling. I know that's not really true but . . . when I see you in so much pain I don't know what to do. I don't want you to be so fucking miserable. When you talk about the cats I can't stand it.
>
> *H:* (Still tearful.) I don't want to repeat what happened to Mom and Dad. Maybe that's why I cried so hard . . . I don't know how I will ever be able to break that cycle. I tried so hard. I don't know how I could have tried any harder.
>
> *T:* Maybe trying harder is counterproductive . . . tell me more about the trap you feel you are in.

The therapist is, at this point, trying to allow the couple to share their painful feelings. After allowing Matthew to express his feelings, the therapist shares how he can be helpful.

> *T:* The trap part I can help you with, and trying to change the ways in which you relate—I can help with that. I can coach you on that and help you make the changes you want. I can help you with the sense of loss and helplessness. These are areas in which I can be supportive. We can set up a contract to work on the issues. I can set up a contract with you also, Josephine.

The therapist spends the next ten to fifteen minutes encouraging and allowing the spouses to share their feelings. He then shifts and helps the couple make some initial decisions about practical aspects regarding the separation. He shares with them the feelings that they can expect to experience in the next several months and the importance of handling the divorce in a mature way. He concludes with establishing a contract for divorce therapy.

The case of Matthew and Josephine illustrates the painful process of divorce. Spouses lose confidence, feel helpless and fear the future. The therapist must encourage the partners to deal directly with issues rather than block or run away from them. By working through these issues, they maximize the opportunity to regain autonomy. They are then able to structure a foundation for a new single life, one which will be strong enough to eventually invite in a new partner.

This case also shows how, without the binding force of mutual love, a marriage can fall, no matter how hard one partner tries to hold it up. Love cannot be bought, bargained for, or negotiated. It must be experienced, freely given and freely received.

REFERENCES
AND SUGGESTED
BIBLIOGRAPHY

REFERENCES

1. U. S. Bureau of the Census, Current-Population Reports, Series P-20, No. 433. "Marital Status and Living Arrangement, "March 1988, p. 59.
2. Saxton, Lloyd, *The Individual, Marriage, and the Family,* Belmont, California: Wadsworth, 1977, p. 9.
3. Fromm, Eric, *The Art of Loving.* New York: Harper and Rowe, 1956
4. O. Henry, *The Gift of the Magi.* Indiana: Bobbs-Merrill, 1978.
5. Nouwen, Henri, J. M., *Out of Solitude: Three Meditations on the Christian Life.* Indiana: Ave Maria Press, 1974, p. 57.
6. Bell, Charles, *Modern Love Poems.* "The Fire." D&J Kliener, New York: Doubleday, 1961
7. Johnson, Robert A., *We: Understanding the Psychology of Romantic Love.* San Francisco: Harper and Rowe, 1983.
8. Nabokov, Vladimir, V., *Lectures on Russian Literature,* "Anna Karenin," (Ed.) Fredson Bowers, New York: Harcourt and Brace, 1980.
9. Becker, Howard and Barnes, Harry E., *Social Thought From Lore to Science.* New York: Dove Pub., Inc., 1961, p. 59.
10. Bowen, Murray, *Family Therapy in Clinical Practice,* New York: Dove Pub, Inc., 1968.
11. Rhodes, Sonya, L., "A Developmental Approach to the Life Cycle of the Family," *Social Casework,* 58:301–312, 1977.
12. *Omini,* Omini Pub.: New York, March, Vol. 10, No. 3, p. 108.
13. Tolstoy, Leo, *Anna Karenina.* New York: Bantam Books, 1981, p. 1

14. Frasier, J. Scott, "Structured and Strategic Family Therapy: A Basis for Marriage or Grounds for Divorce," *Journal of Marriage and Family Therapy,* 8:13–22, 1982. Liddle, Howard, A., "On the Problem of Eclecticism: A Call for Epistemologic Clarifications and Human Scale Theories," *Family Process,* 21:243–250, 1982., Zuk, Gerald, R., "Family Therapy: Clinical Hodgepodge or Clinical Science?" *Journal of Marriage and Family Counseling,* 2:299–304, 1976.

15. Proschaska, James and Proschaska, Janice, "Twentieth Century Trends in Marriage and Marital Therapy," in Paolino, Thomas, J. and McGrady, Barbara S., (Eds.), *Marriage and Marital Therapy,* New York: Brunner Mazel, 1978, p. 12–15.

16. The stages of the initial interview are an expanded version of the ones developed by Jay Haley in Haley, Jay, *Problem Solving Therapy: New Strategies for Effective Family Therapy,* San Francisco, Jossey-Bass, 1976.

17. Robinson, Edwin A., Collected Poems, "Eros Turrance," New York: The MacMillan Co, 1921.

18. Dickinson, Emily, *LXIX,* Poems by Emily Dickinson, Bianchi, Martha, D. (Ed.), Boston: Little, Brown and Co., 1957.

19. Kaslow, Florence W., "Divorce and Divorce Therapy," in Gurman, A. S. and Kniskern, D. P. (Eds.), *Handbook of Family Therapy,* New York: Brunner/Mazel, 1981, p. 672–674.

SUGGESTED BIBLIOGRAPHY

Ables, Billie S., *Therapy for Couples,* San Francisco, California: Jossey-Bass, 1977.

Anderson, Carol M, *Mastering Resistance: A Practical Guide to Family Therapy,* New York, The Guilford Press, 1983.

Bagarozzi, Dennis A. and Wodaraski, John S., "A Social Exchange Typology of Conjugal Relationships and Conflict Development," in *Journal of Marriage and Family Counseling,* 3:53–60, 1977.

Baucom, Donald H. and Epstein Norman, *Cognitive-Behavioral Marital Therapy,* New York, Brunner/Mazel, 1990.

Beavers, W. Robert, *Successful Marriage: A Family Systems Approach to Couples Therapy,* New York, W. W. Norton and Co. 1985.

Bell, John E., *Family Therapy,* New York, Jason Aronson, 1975.

Berger, Milton M. (ed.), *Beyond the Double Bind: Communication and Family*

Systems, Theories, and Techniques with Schizophrenics, New York, Brunner Mazel, 1978.

Bernal, Guillermo and Baker, Jeffrey, "Toward a Metacommuncational Framework of Couples Interactions," *Family Process,* 18:293–302,1979.

Bockus, Frank, *Couple Therapy,* New York, Jason Aronson, 1980.

Boszormenyi-Nagy and Spark, Geraldine M., *Invisible Loyalties,* New York, Harper and Row, Pub., 1973.

Bowen, Murray, *Family Therapy in Clinical Practice,* New York, Jason Aronson, 1978.

Bross, Allon (ed.) *Family Therapy: Principles of Strategic Practice,* New York, The Guilford Press, 1983.

Carter, Elizabeth A. and McGoldrick, Monica (eds.), *The Family Life Cycle: A Framework for Family Therapy,* New York, Gardner Press, 1980.

Cookerly, J. Richard, "Does Marital Therapy Do Any Lasting Good?" in *Journal of Marital and Family Therapy,* 6:393–398, 1980.

Crosby, John F. (ed.) *When One Wants Out and the Other Doesn't: Doing Therapy With Polarized Couples,* New York, Brunner/Mazel, 1 9 8 9.

Dayringer, Richard, "Fair-Fight for Change: A Therapeutic Use of Aggressiveness in Couple Counseling," in *Journal of Marriage and Family Counseling,* 2:115–130, 1976.

Elbaum, Phillip L., "The Dynamics, Implications and Treatment of Extramarital Sexual Relationships for the Family Therapist," in *Journal of Marital and Family Therapy,* 7:489–496, 1981.

Elbow, Margaret, "Theoretical Considerations of Violent Marriages," in *Social Casework,* 58:515–526, 1977.

Ellis, Albert, "Techniques of Handling Anger in Marriage," in *Journal of Marriage and Family Counseling,* 2:305–316, 1976.

Feldman, Larry R., "Depression and Marital Interaction," in *Family Process,* 15:389–396, 1976.

Feldman, Larry R., "Marital Conflict and Marital Intimacy," An Integrative Psychodynamic-Behavioral-Systemic Model," in *Family Process,* 18:69–78, 1979.

Figley, Charles, R., *Helping Traumatized Families,* San Francisco, California, Jossey-Bass Pub., 1989.

Framo, James L, *Explorations in Marital and Family Therapy,* New York, Springer Pub., 1982.

Fraser, J. Scott, "Structural and Strategic Family Therapy: A Basis for Marriage or Grounds for Divorce?" in *Journal of Marital and Family Therapy,* 8:13–22, 1982.

Goldberg, Daniel C. (Ed.), *Contemporary Marriage: Special Issues in Couple Therapy,* Homewood, Illinois, The Dorsey Press, 1985.

Greenberg, Leslie S. and Johnson, Susan M., *Emotionally Focused Therapy for Couples,* New York, The Guilford Press, 1988.

Greer, Steven E. and D'Zurilla, "Behavioral Approaches to Marital Discord and Conflict," in *Journal of Marriage and Family Counseling,* 1:299–316, 1975.

Gurman, Alan, S., *Questions and Answers in the Practice of Family Therapy, V. I and V. II,* New York, Brunner/Mazel, 1981.

Gurman, Alan, S. and Kniskern, D. P., (Eds.), *Handbook of Family Therapy,* New York, Brunner/Mazel, 1981.

Hale, B. John, "Gestalt Techniques in Marriage Counseling," in *Social Casework,* 59:428–433, 1978.

Haley, Jay, *Ordeal Therapy,* New York, Jossey-Bass, Pub., 1981.

Haley, Jay and Hoffman, Lynn, *Techniques of Family Therapy,* New York, Basic Books, Inc., 1967.

Hoffman, Lynn, *Foundations of Family Therapy: A Conceptual Framework for Systems Change,* New York, Basic Books, Inc., 1981.

Horewitz, James, S., *Family Therapy and Transactional Analysis,* New York, Jason Aronson.

Im, Won-Gi, Wilner, R. Stefanie, and Breit, Miranda, "Jealousy: Intervention in Couple Therapy," in *Family Process,* 22:211–220, 1983.

Imber-Black, Evan, Roberts, Janine, and Whiting, Richard, *Rituals in Families and Family Therapy,* New York, W. W. Norton and Co., 1988.

Jacobson, Neil, S., "Beyond Empiricism: The Politics of Marital Therapy," *Family Process,* 22:211–220, 1983.

Jacobson, Neil, S. and Margolin Gayla, *Marital Therapy,* New York, Brunner/ Mazel, Pub., 1979.

Jurg, Willi, *Couples in Collusion,* New York, Jason Aronson, 1975.

Kaslow, Florence and Schwartz Lita, L., *The Dynamics of Divorce: A Life Cycle Perspective,* New York, Brunner/Mazel, 1987.

Lang, Alfred, Van Der Hart, Onno, *Directive Family Therapy,* New York, Brunner/Mazel, 1983.

Lazarus, Arnold, "Divorce Counseling or Marriage Therapy? A Therapeutic Option," in *Journal of Marital and Family Therapy,* 7:12–22, 1981.

Lazarus, Arnold A., *The Practice of Multi-Model Therapy,* New York, McGraw/ Hill, 1981.

Lester, Gregory W., Beckham, Ernest, and Baucom, Donald H., "Implementation of Behavioral Marital Therapy," in *Journal of Marital and Family Therapy,* 2:189–200., 1980.

Liddle, I., Howard A., "On the Problem of Eclecticism: A Call for Epistemologic Clarification and Human-Scale Theories," in *Family Process,* 21:243–250, 1982.

Liebman, Ronald, Honig, Paul and Berger, Henry, "An Integrated Treatment Program for Psychogenic Pain," in *Family Process,* 15:397–406, 1976.

Luther, Grace and Loev, Irv, "Resistance in Marital Therapy," in *Journal of Marital and Family,* 7:475–480, 1981.

Mace, David R., "Marital Intimacy and the Deadly Love-Anger Cycle," in *Journal of Marriage and Family Counseling,* 2:131–138, 1976.

Martin, Peter A, *A Marital Therapy Manual,* New York, Brunner/Mazel, 1976.

McGoldrick, Monica, Anderson, Carol M. and Walsh, Froma, (Eds.) *Women in Families: A Framework for Family Therapy,* New York, W. W. Norton and Co., 1989.

McMullin, Rian E., *Handbook of Cognitive Therapy Techniques,* New York, W. W. Norton and Co., 1986.

Minuchin, Salvador, *Family and Family Therapy,* Cambridge, Mass., Harvard University Press, 1978.

Minuchin, Salvador, *Families of the Slums: An Exploration of Their Structure and Treatment,* New York, Basic Books, Inc. 1967.

Minuchin, Salvador and Fishman H. Charles, *Family Therapy Techniques,* Cambridge, Mass., Harvard University Press, 1981.

Murphy, James M., "A Tandem Approach: Marriage Counseling as Process in Tandem with Individual Psychotherapy," in *Journal of Marriage and Family Counseling,* 2:13–22, 1976.

Napier, Augustus Y. with Whitaker, Carl A., *The Family Crucible,* New York, Harper and Row, Pub., 1978.

Neill, John, R. and Kniskern, David, P. *From Psyche to System: The Evolving Therapy of Carl Whitaker,* New York, The Guilford Press, 1982.

Nichols, Michael P. and Schwartz, Richard C., *Family Therapy: Concepts and Methods,* Boston, Allyn and Bacon, 1991.

Olson, David and Assoc., *Families: What Makes Them Work,* Beverly Hills, California, Sage Pub., 1983.

Overturf, Joan, "Marital Therapy: Toleration of Differentness," in *Journal of Marriage and Family Counseling,* 2:235–242, 1976.

Palazzoli, Mara S., Cecchin, Gianfranco, and Assoc., *Paradox and Counterparadox: A New Model in the Therapy of the Family in Schizophrenic Transaction,* New York, Jason Aronson, 1978.

Paolino, Thomas J. and McGrady, Barbara S., *Marriage and Marital Therapy,* New York, Brunner/Mazel, 1978.

Pearce, John K, and Friedman, Leonard J., *Family Therapy: Combining Psychodynamics and Family Systems Approaches,* New York, Grune and Stratton, 1980.

Pittman, Frank, *Private Lies: Infidelity and the Betrayal of Intimacy,* New York, W. W. Norton and Co., 1989.

Rosenberg, John B., "Two is Better Than One: Use of Behavioral Techniques Within a Structural Family Therapy Model," in *Journal of Marriage and Family Counseling,* 4:31–40, 1978.

Sager, Clifford J., Brown, Hollis, S. and Assoc., *Treating Remarried Family,* New York, Brunner/Mazel, 1983.

Satir, Virginia, *Conjoint Family Therapy,* Palo Alto, Calif., Science and Behavior Books, 1972.

Sherman, Robert, and Fredman, Norman, *Handbook of Structured Techniques in Marriage and Family Therapy,* New York, Brunner/Mazel, 1986.

Spinks, Suzanne H., and Birchler, Gary, "Behavioral Systems Marital Therapy: Dealing with Resistance, in *Family Process,* 21:169–186, 1982.

Stanton, M. Duncan, "An Integrated Structural/Strategic Approach to Family Therapy," in *Journal of Marital and Family Therapy,* 7:427–440, 1981.

Startz, Morton, R. and Evans, Claire W., "Developmental Phases of Marriage and Marital Therapy," in *Social Casework,* 62:343–351, 1981.

Strayhorn, Joseph Mr. Jr., "Social Exchange Theory: Cognitive Restructuring in Marital Therapy," in *Family Process,* 17:437448, 1978.

Strong, John R., "A Marital Conflict Resolution Model: Redefining Conflict to Achieve Intimacy," in *Journal of Marriage and Family Counseling,* 1:269–276, 1975.

Stuart, Richard B., *Helping Couples Change: A Social Learning Approach to Marital Therapy,* New York, The Guilford Press, 1980.

Tannen, Deborah, *You Just Don't Understand: Women and men in Conversation,* New York, William Morrow and Co., Inc., 1990.

Tsoi-Hoshmand, Lisa, "Marital Therapy: An Integrative Behavioral-Learning Model," in *Journal of Marriage and Family Counseling,* 2:179–192, 1976.

Wallace, Marquis E., "A Focal Conflict Model of Marital Disorders, in *Social Casework,* 7:423–429, 1979.

Walters, Marianne, Carter, Betty and Assoc. *The Invisible Web: Gender Patterns in Family Relationships,* New York, The Guilford Press, 1988.

Watzlawick, Paul, Weakland, John, et al., *Change,* New York, W. W. Norton, 1974.

Weeks, Gerald R. (Ed.), *Treating Couples: The Intersystem Model of the Marriage Council of Philadelphia,* New York, Brunner/Mazel, 1989.

Weeks, Gerald R. and L'Abate, Luciano, *Paradoxical Psychotherapy: Theory and Practice with Individuals, Couples and Families,* New York, Brunner/Mazel, 1982.

Wile, Daniel B., "An Insight Approach to Marital Therapy," in *Journal of Marital and Family Therapy,* 5:43–52, 1979.

Zuk, Gerald R., "Family Therapy: Clinical Hodgepodge or Clinical Science?" in *Journal of Marriage and Family Counseling,* 4:299304, 1976.

INDEX